12.73

Aniela Jaffé

Was C.G. Jung a Mystic?

and other essays

"'Was C.G.Jung a Mystic?' and other essays" by Aniela Jaffé; translated by Diana Dachler and Fiona Cairns; edited by Robert Hinshaw, assisted by Gary Massey and Henriette Wagner. Cover design by Adrienne Pearson, typesetting by Henriette and Götz Wagner.

ISBN 3 85630 – 508 – 4

CONTENTS

Foreword

After Aniela Jaffé's memorable collaboration with C.G. Jung on his life story, *Memories, Dreams, Reflections*[1] and painstaking work on his *Letters*,[2] and after her illustrated Jung biography, *Word and Image*,[3] and *The Myth of Meaning*,[4] among other efforts, it is a pleasure to be able to present a new selection of essays from her prolific German writings, many of which still remain to be translated. All four of the essays in this volume are published here for the first time in English.

The title piece, "Was C.G. Jung a Mystic?," the author's latest contribution, appears for the first time in any language. As in Frau Jaffé's other writings, she here approaches the life and work of her subject from many angles, providing insights which are the rich fruit of her long years of close association with Jung.

---

1 *Memories, Dreams, Reflections by C.G. Jung*, recorded and edited by Aniela Jaffé (transl. R. and C. Winston), Pantheon, New York, 1962.

2 *C.G. Jung: Letters*, edited in German by Aniela Jaffé and in English by Gerhard Adler, transl. by R.F.C. Hull, Princeton and Routledge and Kegan Paul, New York and London, 1973–75.

3 *C.G. Jung: Word and Image*, edited by Aniela Jaffé, Princeton, 1977.

4 Aniela Jaffé, *The Myth of Meaning*, orig. 1970, 4th edition Daimon, Zürich, 1986.

"The Romantic Period in Germany" consists of a key chapter from Aniela Jaffé's untranslated literary work, *Bilder und Symbole aus E.T.A. Hoffmanns Märchen 'Der goldne Topf'*[5] *(Images and Symbols in E.T.A. Hoffmann's Tale, 'The Golden Pot')*. This major effort of some 380 pages occupied her for more than ten years before its publication in 1950 along with essays by C.G. Jung in a volume entitled, *Gestaltungen des Unbewussten* (Figures of the Unconscious).[6]

"The Individuation of Mankind" was originally presented in German as a paper at the Eranos Conference in Ascona in 1974, and subsequently published in the Eranos Yearbook.[7]

The fourth and last essay in this collection, "Transcendence", based on her conversations about post-mortal existence with C.G. Jung in the final months of his life, was written in 1985 and published for the first time in Aniela Jaffé's recent book in German, *Themen bei C.G. Jung*.[8]

This latest little collection of essays, written over a period of nearly half a century, is at once both 'modern' and timeless, and it is highly appropriate that these writings by Aniela Jaffé also become available to readers of English.

Robert Hinshaw

---

5 Aniela Jaffé, *Bilder und Symbole aus E.T.A. Hoffmanns Märchen 'Der goldne Topf,'* orig. 1950, 3rd ed. Daimon, Einsiedeln, 1986.

6 C.G. Jung and Aniela Jaffé, *Gestaltungen des Unbewussten,* Rascher, Zürich, 1950.

7 Eranos-Jahrbuch 43, Adolf Portmann and Rudolf Ritsema, Editors, Brill, Leiden, 1974.

8 Aniela Jaffé, *Themen bei C.G. Jung,* Daimon, Zürich, 1985.

Was C.G. Jung a Mystic ?

C.G. Jung did not like to be regarded as a mystic: he preferred to be recognized as an empiricist, i.e., a scientist whose research is based on a careful observation of facts. In this sense, he thought of himself as a natural scientist. One can understand why Jung disliked being included in the ranks of mystics when one considers that in his time, and essentially also today, to characterize a scientific author as "mystic" casts a doubt on the reliability or validity of his ideas and his work. Mystical statements are not to be included in the natural sciences. Nevertheless, the clear analogies that exist between mysticism and Jungian psychology cannot be overlooked, and this fact in no way denies its scientific basis.

If the concept "mystic" suggests the immediate experience of the numinous or the perceiving of an originally hidden transcendent reality, the "other side", then it involves an experience which also plays a central role in Jung's approach to analytical psychology; that is, the consideration of images and contents which enter into consciousness from the hidden background of the psyche, the collective unconscious. Nevertheless one must bear in mind that Jung's language and his scientific ideas differ from the language of the mystics, and this difference is significant. Whereas the mystic is content with his belief in the objectivity of his experience, these experiences are subjected by Jung to a critical examination. By taking into account the fundamental science of knowledge (Immanuel Kant's erkenntnis-theoretische Differenzierung), he established the basis for the inclusion of his observations in the science of psychology. According to this view, one proceeds from the fact that the background of the psyche, the collective unconscious, must be conceived of as a realm with neither space nor time that eludes any objective knowledge. What we perceive are its effects. In itself, it remains concealed, unknowable. "The concept of the unconscious *posits nothing,* it designates only my *unknowing,*" wrote Jung in a letter[1] and elsewhere he states, "The unconscious is a piece of Nature our mind cannot comprehend."[2]

The concept of the collective unconscious has passed into general usage, just as the concept of its contents, the archetypes. So let us stress one fact essential to our questioning but which is often overlooked and has therefore become a source of misunderstanding. Jung distinguished between the unknowable archetypes in the hidden impenetrable realm of the unconscious and the com-

---

1 *Letters, I,* (Feb 8, 1946 Frischknecht).

2 *Letters, II,* (May 3, 1958 Kelsey).

prehensible archetypal images and contents structured by them that can be recognized in dreams, fairy tales, works of art, religions and so forth. It was the similarity or inner relatedness of such images in myths and in cultures of all times that had originally led him to presuppose the existence of a common transpersonal denominator: the archetypes. By this he meant inborn dispositions that play a role in the realm of the psychic, in the same way as the structuring instincts in the realm of the biological. One could also say the archetypes are "spiritual instincts."

Scientific psychology is limited to the observation and study of accessible archetypal images and contents, in other words, human assertions that nevertheless may not be taken to be objective knowledge about what transcends consciousness: the metaphysical. They remain in the human-psychic realm. Jung spoke of "psychic facts." He restricted his research to these, and in so doing continually stressed the importance of the epistemological limitation formulated by Kant. Insofar as his research was limited to these "facts," he was justified in calling himself an empiricist.

The archetypes as such, contents of the collective unconscious, remain unknowable and removed from the reach of objective scientific research. Still, it is a valid hypothesis that the archetypal images, as symbols, refer to the incognizable transcendental archetypes, by which they are themselves structured. In this way they build a bridge between consciousness and the unconscious.

It is known that the natural sciences have also arrived at the boundary of the objectively knowable.[3] They also recognize a "boundless mysterious field" behind all life (Adolf Portmann), a "transcendental and autonomous order," to which "the psyche of the observer, as well as that which can be observed" are subordinate. (W. Pauli)

The strict and conscious observance of the epistemological limitation leads the natural sciences as well as psychology to the acceptance of an incomprehensible background realm that is without space and time. Throughout the ages human beings have longed to penetrate its secret and make it accessible. Thus the splendid body of metaphysical thought, the content of mysticism, and of religions came into being. As images and contents created by man they bear witness to an immeasurable richness of the soul. Thus, according to Jung, "It is the psyche which, by the divine creative power inherent in it, makes the metaphysical assertion ... not only is it the condition of all metaphysical reality, it *is* that reality."[4]

Jung himself refused to make any statement about the transcendental background, except to say that it exists. In his words, "That the world inside and outside ourselves rests on a transcendental background is as certain as our own existence."[5] That this background remains hidden

---

3 Cf. "Ordering Factors in Nature," *The Myth of Meaning*, Aniela Jaffé, 1984.

4 *Psychology and Religion: West and East*, C.W. XI, par. 836.

5 *Memories, Dreams, Reflections by C.G. Jung*, recorded and edited by Aniela Jaffé (transl. R. and C. Winston), Pantheon, New York, 1962, p. 305. Hereafter referred to as *Memories*.

does not reduce its significance. One could say: quite the contrary. For Jung, precisely the inability to "know" in this connection signified, in his own words, a richness and a treasure that he sought always to preserve. An ethical researcher can acknowledge when he reaches the end of his knowledge, as this end is "the beginning of a higher wisdom." The incomprehensible nature of something that is nevertheless effective imparts the sense of a *Mysterium* that transcends the human and simultaneously encompasses him.

These brief comments serve only as a necessary sketch of the psychic structure. The real question posed here is: how does the individual experience the unconscious? And how does he experience the archetypes or the archetypal contents, the symbols?

The immediate experience of archetypal contents is by no means an everyday event, and in most cases the individual reacts with deepest emotion, occasionally with fear. Two examples will show that the emotion springs from a feeling of helplessness on the part of the individual or ego-personality with respect to forces that arise from his own psyche, but which he none the less cannot control. Without his cooperation, without his willing it, archetypal images emerge from a realm that transcends consciousness and work their powerful effects. They seem to be characterized by an intentionality, a dynamism or an autonomy, and it is this which lends to them the deeply moving character of the numinous, comparable to the experience of a demonic or godly might.

Jung once described "A Protestant theologian (who) dreamt repeatedly that he stood on a cliff; below lay a deep valley and in it a dark lake. He knew in the dream, that until now something had always prevented him from approaching the lake. This time, however, he decided to go down to the water. As he neared the shore, it became dark and uncanny, and suddenly a gust of wind blew over the surface of the water. A panic fear gripped him then, and he awoke."[6]

Jung interpreted the dream in the following way: the climbing down to the lake means that the dreamer has descended into his own depths. What grips him and causes him to panic is hardly the dream image as such, as it is a very simple one: a gust of wind blows over the water. The numinosity of the picture corresponds much more to the autonomous dynamism of the effective but unknowable archetype. In the dream it manifests itself as a breath of the spirit "that bloweth where it listeth," (John 3:8) "But this is uncanny, like everything of which we are not the cause nor know the cause. It hints at an unseen presence, a numen to which neither human expectations nor the machinations of the will have given life. It lives of itself, and a shudder runs through the man who thought that 'spirit' was merely what he believes, what he makes himself, what is said in books, or what people talk about. But when it happens spontaneously it is a spookish thing, and primitive fear seizes the naive mind."

---

6 *The Archetypes of the Collective Unconscious,* C.W. IX i, par. 34.

The fear associated with the experience is a frequent first reaction to an encounter with the archetypal contents. Because of their autonomy, also perhaps because of their strangeness, they cannot be accepted by consciousness as a content of one's own psyche. Man experiences fear when confronted with something overpowering, which in the deepest sense is part of him, and to which he belongs.

The second example shows the autonomous nature of contents emerging from the unconscious. It is the story of a patient, an academic, who was afflicted with severe anxiety neurosis. He suffered from an imaginary carcinoma, even though the best doctors had assured him again and again that he was completely healthy. The man knew that the doctors were right, still, the "invader," the autonomous agent, proved itself to be stronger than objective medical truth and his own reason. The fear always returned, so that one had to ask: what demonic power was at work here? And, why was he chastened by this fear of death? In the course of therapy the unconscious psychic and religious sources of his fear were raised to consciousness, whereupon the tormenting fantasy disappeared.

These examples show the effect of archetypal forces arising out of the unconscious: the ego-personality is gripped by them and experiences the autonomous sovereignty of the non-ego. Because of this numinous autonomy Jung attributed a fundamental significance to such experiences. Ultimately they are not distinguishable from that superiority or that "compelling numinosity" that man since time immemorial has called "God," or the "Godhead."

In numerous places in his work, Jung discussed the indistinguishability of the godhead and the unconscious. His thoughts on this subject build the bridge to mysticism. Two quotations might serve as illustration. The first more or less deals with the designation of the autonomous agent as "God." It comes from a letter written when Jung was 85 years old in connection with the BBC television series, "Face to Face." Jung was asked by the interviewer whether he believed in God, whereupon, after a slight hesitation, he answered, "I do not believe, I know." As a result of this he received a flood of letters that referred to the words, "I know," and wanted to learn more about this. The following quotation is taken from one of his replies:

> "The experience which I call God is the experience of my own will with respect to another often very much stronger will that crosses my path with apparently disastrous results, in that it puts strange thoughts in my head, occasionally determines or defines my fate in most unwished-for ways, or, gives it an unexpectedly favorable turn quite independent of my own knowledge and my intentions. This strange force intervening against or for my conscious intentions is well known to me. For this reason I say, 'I know Him.' But why do you want to call this thing 'God?' To that I ask: 'Why not?' It was always called 'God.' Truly an excellent and suitable name. Who could in complete seriousness maintain that his fate and his life proceed entirely according to his

own conscious plans? Do we possess a complete picture of the world? In reality there are a million assumptions and situations that are removed from our control. There are innumerable opportunities for our life to take another direction. Those who claim to be masters of their own destinies are as a rule slaves of fate ... what I would like, that I know; but I hesitate and doubt whether that 'something' shares in my intention or not."[7]

It is no contradiction when Jung in another place said that he did not associate that superior and autonomous power which he here termed "God," with any specific confession, nor ascribe to it any definite characteristic at all. It is neither good nor evil, neither active nor passive, neither personal nor impersonal. Man attributes such characteristics to the archetypal *image of God.* God is not touched by them. God was and remained for Jung a "transcendental mystery," the "mystery of all mysteries."[8] He formulated somewhat drastically in a letter, "When I say God I mean an anthropo-morphic (archetypal) God-image and do not imagine I have said anything about God."[9] To a young woman he wrote, "One must always remember that God is a mystery, and everything we say on the subject is said and believed by human beings. We make images and concepts, and when I speak of God I always mean the image man has made of Him. But no one

---

7 *Letters, II,* (Nov 16, 1959 Brooke).

8 *Letters, I,* (Dec 31, 1949 White).

9 *Letters, II,* (Apr 23, 1952 Haberlandt).

knows what He is like or he would be a god himself."[10]

In spite of this epistemological limitation Jung consistently professed the acceptance of a metaphysical although unknowable God. "I don't by any means dispute the existence of a metaphysical God. I permit myself, however, to put human statements under the microscope."[11] As a scientist and empiricist he confined himself to the investigation of human assertions about the religious, about God, and grounded his psychology of religion on the interpretation and comparison of these facts. The metaphysical God, "God Himself," remained untouched.

It might serve here to summarize what has been said up until now: the unconscious is a hidden, transcendental realm of being, an incognizable reality. It is the autonomy and sovereignty of the forces arising out of it that lend numinosity to them, with the result that man labels them "godly."

> "Recognizing that they do not spring from his conscious personality, he calls them mana, daimon, or God. Science employs the term 'the unconscious,' thus admitting that it knows nothing about it, for it can know nothing about the substance of the psyche when the sole means of knowing anything *is* the psyche. Therefore the validity of such terms as mana, daimon, or God can be neither disproved nor affirmed. We can, however, establish that the

---

10 *Letters, II,* (Aug 17, 1957 Roswitha N.).

11 *Letters, II,* (May 5, 1952 Buri).

sense of strangeness connected with the experience of something objective, apparently outside the psyche, is indeed authentic ... However I prefer the term 'the unconscious' knowing that I might equally well speak of 'God' or 'daimon' if I wished to express myself in mythic language. When I do use such mythic language, I am aware that 'mana,' 'daimon,' and 'God' are synonyms for the unconscious – that is to say, we know just as much or just as little about them.'"[12]

It would nevertheless be a mistake if one were to conclude from the impossibility of distinguishing between "godhead" and "unconscious," or to conclude from their synonymity that Jung assumed the two factors were identical – one of the most frequent misunderstandings regarding his psychology of religion. The indistinguishability applies only to the experience, not to that which is experienced. Jung formulated carefully: "This is certainly not to say that what we call the unconscious is identical with God or set up in his place. It is simply the medium from which religious experience seems to flow. As to what the further cause of such experience may be, the answer to this lies beyond the range of human knowledge. Knowledge of God is a transcendental problem."[13] Although godhead and unconscious in subjective experience cannot be distinguished from one another, they may not, as factors in themselves, be seen as identical with one another. However,

12 *Memories*, p. 336.

13 *Civilization in Transition*, C.W. X, "Self Knowledge," par. 565.

there results from the incomprehensibility of both God and the unconscious, as well as out of their numinous autonomy, a correspondence or synonymity between the two concepts.

Both Jungian psychology and mysticism deal with the experience of the numinous. The difference is that mysticism speaks of an encounter with God and lets the matter rest at that. Jungian psychology also speaks of an encounter with God, in the sense that "God" represents the word or the designation for something incognizable and incomprehensible. For both, "God" is a primordial human experience and in this sense the assertion of St. Augustine that "self-knowledge paves the way to the knowledge of God" held great meaning also for Jung. He liked to quote his words, "Go not outside, look into thyself: Truth dwells in the inner man." Master Eckhart went so far as to compare the soul to the godhead: he said, "For the soul is created equal with the Godhead."

Jung formulated the same thought more cautiously: "It would be going perhaps too far to speak of an affinity; but at all events the soul must contain in itself the faculty of relationship to God, i.e., a correspondence, otherwise a connection could never come about. This correspondence is, in psychological terms, the archetype of the God-image." It enables the soul to be an eye destined to see the light, for "As the eye to the sun, so the soul corresponds to God."[14]

Instead of the "archetypal image of God" Jung could also have written: the archetypal image of

---

[14] Cf. *Psychology and Alchemy*, C.W. XII, par. 11.

wholeness (the Self) corresponds to the essence of God, because empirically, images of wholeness and images of God are not always distinguishable from one another. Here a synonymity also exists. The various representations of unity, for example, as anthropos, creator, light, word, trinity, quaternity, circle, sphere and so forth are similarly old and revered symbols of God. And when Paul wrote about "Christ in me," the son of God must also be understood as a symbol of the Self in this sense, as the innermost core of the personality, in which the personality is at the same time contained. With respect to the indistinguishability of the concept "God" and unconscious mentioned earlier, the accent must be put on the incognizable and effective, on that which, for example, the biologists designated as the "mysterious ground," and the physicists as the "transcendent principle." As regards the indistinguishability of the symbols of the Self and the symbols of God, the accent lies on a relationship of the individual to the numinous, to the godhead.

In recognizing a correspondence between the Self and the godhead, Jungian psychology represents an amplification with respect to the assertions and teachings of mysticism. The mystical experience must be understood in a new sense: according to definition the central archetype of the Self is an embodiment of the totality, "a sum of the conscious and the unconscious psyche."[15] But this is not a sufficient description. As with any archetype, a dynamic is inherent in the Self, and this autonomous force directs a process which

---

[15] Ibid., par. 247.

Jung named the *process of individuation.* The inner or psychic aspect of this individuation process reveals itself in images or series of images that are structured by the archetype of the Self and are perceived by consciousness. Its necessary completion or equivalent is outer reality; that is, its unfolding in individuality, in the fate or destiny of the individual. For this reason individuation fulfills itself meaningfully only in everyday existence. Both aspects of the process, the inner and the outer, are structured by the mighty archetype of the Self. Individuation is its realization in space and time. The mission of the individual, or his ego-personality, which stands between the inner and the outer aspects, lies in ever-renewed, because always required, attempts to unite the inner pictures and the outer reality. In other words: it lies in the effort "to make that which fate intends entirely one's own intention." (Bergengruen)

In the realization of the Self Jung saw the meaning of life: "Every carrier is charged with an individual destiny and destination, and the realization of these alone makes sense of life."[16] This is a very prosaic description; its significance is apparent only when one considers that the archetype realizing itself in existence is the Self, a numen, an originally "nameless ineffable." For this reason individuation fulfills itself not in the fullest life lived for its own sake, not in deepening self-awareness; rather, its meaning arises from the numinosity of the Self. Individuation must be understood in religious language as the realization of the "godly" in the human, as the fulfilling

16 Ibid., par. 330.

of a "godly mission." The conscious experience of life becomes a religious experience, one could just as well say, a mystical experience.

Repeatedly, and with justification, the question is asked as to whether there is also a natural or unconscious individuation. This question must be answered in the affirmative. Individuation also fulfills itself when the world of the unconscious remains in darkness and no archetypal image is perceived, let alone recognized in its implications.

To illustrate this, Jung took the development processes in nature: out of the crystal lattice develops the crystal, out of the acorn, the oak, out of the egg, the bird: it is always a preordained form that develops in the course of life. Or, as Jung wrote in a letter, "Everything living dreams individuation, for everything strives toward its own wholeness."[17]

Nevertheless, only the lending of depth to outer reality through knowledge of its background leads to a mystical experience. In Jung's judgment: "Life that just happens in and for itself is not real life; it is real only when it is *known*,"[18] and these words also contain the challenge to an expansion of consciousness.

By rendering conscious the transpersonal influence on our psyches, through the experience of its numinosity, forces are recognized which underlie one's being and behavior in a structuring and autonomous way, as well as being behind the apparently random unfolding of events. One ex-

---

[17] *Letters, II,* (Apr 23, 1949 Stamm).

[18] Ibid., par. 105.

periences or senses the wider context in which life is lived, and toward which goal it is striving.

Jung alluded to these matters when he wrote: "You are quite right: the main interest of my work is not concerned with the treatment of neurosis, but rather with the approach to the numinous. But the fact is that the approach to the numinous is the real therapy, and inasmuch as you attain to the numinous experience, you are released from the curse of pathology. Even the very disease takes on a numinous character."[19] In life there is nothing that cannot be understood in the deepest sense as referring to the transcendent; sickness and suffering are no exception. In his psychotherapy or analysis Jung attempted to open the eyes of the individual to this.

The goal of individuation, the actualization of the Self, will never be completely realized. Because of its consciousness-transcending nature, the archetype of the Self can never be fully comprehended, and because of its boundlessness, never fully realized in life. The "successful individuation" is never a total but only an optimal approaching, a "never-ending approximation" of consciousness and the realization of the totality. The ultimate goal remains unattainable and concealed.

"The very impossibility of this task gives it its significance," stated Jung. For as long as the superiority of the individual is not absolutely called in question, something remains unaffected in him. Only in its inferiority does the ego experi-

---

19 *Letters, I,* (Aug 31, 1945 unnamed addressee).

ence the sovereignty of the Self, or, the sovereignty of the numinous.

In this brief description of the concept of individuation a picture is sketched of a reciprocal relationship between the ego and the Self; mythically stated, between man and God.

The archetype of the Self forces its way into consciousness from the unconscious, and the response of the human to this impulse are the archetypal images of God on the one hand, and the living out of fate as a fulfillment of his destiny on the other. The images tend also to reveal the eternal aspect of the Self, its uniqueness as defined by man.

Uniqueness always implies limitation: the individual achieves a sense of the infinite only when he is limited, in the extreme. "The greatest limitation for man is the 'Self,'" wrote Jung. "It is manifested in the experience: 'I am only that!' Only consciousness of our narrow confinement in the Self forms the link to the limitlessness of the unconscious. In such awareness we experience ourselves concurrently as limited and eternal, as both the one and the other. In knowing ourselves to be unique in our personal combination, that is, ultimately limited, we possess also the capacity for becoming conscious of the infinite. But only then!"[20]

Out of the reciprocal relationship between Self and individual, out of the question of the Self and the answer of the individual, ensues in religious language an image of a God who seeks man just

20 *Memories*, p. 325.

as much as He is sought by man. God seeks the individual in order to realize himself in his soul and in his life. Expressed psychologically: the Self requires the ego-personality in order to manifest itself; the ego-personality requires the Self as the origin of its life and as its fate. In religious language this means "God needs man, just as man needs God."

The reciprocal relationship in which God stands opposite man not only as a superior Other, but also as a seeker, a Thou, does not eliminate the inferiority of the human being with respect to transcendent forces, but rather relativizes it with regard to them. Jung expressed this in remarks about prayer in a letter: "I have thought much about prayer. It – prayer – is very necessary because it makes the Beyond we conjecture and think about an immediate reality, and transposes us into the duality of the ego and the dark Other. One hears oneself speaking and can no longer deny that one has addressed "That." The question then arises: What will become of Thee and Me? of the transcendental Thou and the immanent I? The way of the unexpected opens, fearful and unavoidable, with hope of a propitious turn or a defiant 'I will not perish under the will of God unless I myself will it too.' Then only, I feel, is God's will made perfect. Without me it is only his almighty will, a frightful fatality even in its grace, void of sight and hearing, void of knowledge for precisely that reason. I go together with it, an immensely weighty milligram without which God had made his world in vain."[21]

21 *Letters, I,* (Sept 10, 1943 unnamed addressee).

Jung's profession of faith in a creator that has need of man just as much as man has need of the creator corresponds to a picture that is well known from the history of mysticism. Jung especially liked to quote from "The Cherubinic Wanderer" of Angelus Silesius, for example,

> I know that without me God can no moment live;
> were I to die, then He no longer could survive.

or:

> To illuminate my God, the sunshine I must be;
> my beams must radiate his calm and bound less sea.

Master Eckhart, to whose spirit and work Jung felt especially drawn, should also be mentioned here. His words, "That God is God, of this I am a cause," expresses an identical conception of the relationship between God and man.

That God needs man is also a part of the Old Testament heritage. In Isaiah 48:10 it states: "See how I tested you, not as silver is tested, but in the furnace of affliction; there I purified you. For my honour, for my own honour I did it..." Jung recognized the limits of mortal ability to reply to the demand of the Almighty in that he went on, "Man's understanding and will are challenged and can help, but they can never pretend to have plumbed the depths of the spirit and to have quenched the fire raging in it. We can only hope that God, in his grace, will not compel us to go deeper and let ourselves be consumed by his fire."[22]

---

22 *Letters, II,* (Mar 28, 1955 Menz).

Jung did not refer by chance to the words of Isaiah. A dark and gruesome side of the God image emerges from them that makes out of the overwhelming operative a *Tremendum.*

Jung expressed himself in the greatest detail and with deepest emotion on this theme in his work, *Answer to Job.* His ideas brought him close to the mystic Jakob Böhme: "Only when the dark side takes its place beside the light, the will to destroy beside the urge to create, terror beside love, and the world-opposites are seen together in a single image of God, only then does this picture fulfill the requirement of totality."

Let us repeat again that Jung's psychological work deals always with the *image* of God as it reveals itself in the human psyche, not with God himself. To the question about the essence of God, science (psychology) has no answers, but only belief, and as a believer Jung in a letter professed his belief in a god "beyond good and evil," which attests to its incognizable nature.

Jung sees the task of man today in making conscious the "awful dual aspect" of the totality and in enduring it. The fulfilling of this task he termed, in so far as he used religious language, "a service to God," that is, a service which man can provide to God, from which the light in the darkness comes into being. "God is a contradiction in terms, therefore he needs man in order to be made One. God is an ailment man has to cure."[23] Psychologically, this is the suffering called forth by the antinomy in the Self, which must be made

---

23 *Letters, II,* (Jan 5, 1952 Neumann).

conscious and must be united. The uniting of the opposites represented for Jung the real *mysterium conjunctionis.*

Only in the enduring struggle of the individual toward this uniting of the opposites within the Self exists the assurance that he will not fall victim to the light side and succumb to the arrogance of the righteous or evade his destiny. It also prevents him from being overwhelmed by the destructive forces of the unconscious and falling victim to the dark side.

The concept of the uniting of the opposites, in which the unfathomable God requires human help and both God and man work together, is part of the old heritage of Jewish mysticism. It meant a great deal to Jung when, through Gerschom Scholem, he became acquainted with the Kabbala of Isaak Luria (16th century), who had captured these thoughts, which Jung himself valued so highly, in mystical imagery[24]: As the divine light streamed into the primordial space created by God, vessels were created to receive the separate rays, vessels that should catch and preserve them. Yet these proved themselves to be too weak to contain the light and burst asunder. This breaking of the vessels caused the demonic nether-world of evil to come into being. Since then all things carry to a certain extent the flaw within themselves. Redemption lies in the restoration of the original condition before the break, and this process, according to Luria, can be viewed as a perfecting of God. Redemption calls for an impulse which

Broken vessels

---

[24] Cf. Gerschom Scholem, *Die Jüdische Mystik in ihren Hauptströmungen*, 1957, p. 291 ff.

originates not only in God, but also an impulse originating in the creature. Man participates in the cosmic-divine event, in that he in all his deeds attempts to restore the original union. Even his mystical meditation in prayer, which is described as a "descent to the deepest ground of the soul," assists in "uniting the name of God."

In Christian mysticism, it was above all Nicolas of Cusanus who saw the image of God as a union of opposites. Jung concluded his "Psychology of the Transference" with these words: "All the endeavor of our human intellect must be concerned with these deep problems, that is may rise to that simplicity where the opposites coincide."[25]

Jung saw the dignity of man in the fact that he can become conscious of a relationship with the numinous background of the soul; expressed in religious terms, to the godhead. With this, the divine spark becomes "an innermost possession of one's soul." Spontaneous experiences of God happen only to a few. Nevertheless, an individual can succeed to an experience of the numinous if he takes seriously the pictures and dreams arising from the unconscious. Dreams are autonomous messages from the impenetrable background of the soul, which arise independent of one's will. Their often numinous character was emphasized by the theologian John A. Sanford, when he gave his book on the meaning of dreams within the Christian experience the title, "God's Forgotten Language." Jung disagreed with the word "forgotten" and wrote three months before his death,

25 *The Practice of Psychotherapy,* C.W. XVI, par. 537 footnote 29.

that "The voice of God can still be perceived, if one is only humble enough."[26]

Religious experiences belong to the most intimate and personal of human experiences, yet they are of a universal validity and anyone can share in them, since, from a psychological point of view, they are rooted in the collective unconscious and in collective archetypes. The psyche itself possesses a religious function: "*anima naturaliter religiosa*," the soul is religious by nature, formulated Jung according to an old saying. The individual is placed in the middle of the process of revelation. In psychological terms, mystical experiences are exceptional only with regard to their intensity or degree, not in their essence, and that man in his innermost nature was created *homo mysticus*.

Naturally, one cannot argue about the experience of the numinous. Jung wrote, "One can only say that one has never had such an experience, and the other will say: 'Sorry, but I have.' And with this, the discussion comes to an end. It is really of no importance what the world thinks about the religious experience; the one who has had such an experience possesses as a great treasure a thing which will be a source of life, meaning and beauty, and which will lend to the world and humanity a new splendor ... where is the criterion by which such an experience shall be judged invalid and such a faith mere illusion? Is there actually a higher truth regarding ultimate things than that which helps one to live?"[27]

26 *Letters, II,* (Mar 10, 1961 Sanford).

27 *Psychology and Religion: West and East,* C.W. XI, par. 167.

Jung himself had repeated experiences of the numinous in dreams, visions and meditations. They were for him always "experiences of devastating reality," and one could see them as milestones marking his inner development. The inner experience formed part of Jung's life element far more and in a deeper sense than is true for most people. His definition, "God is a primordial experience of man"[28] is also a personal affirmation. In terms of breadth and content his inner experiences surpassed that of his fellow mortals. This could very well be the reason why he and his ideas often appeared strange to others: they are not acquainted with the experiences which underlie Jung's work.

Even as a child, Jung was already extremely receptive to the numinous effects of the archetype. He experienced God as a sovereign will working in him which he confronted in a childlike but serious way, and he experienced Him both in dreams and in tremendous fantasy images which aroused fear and reverence. Looking back when he was 83 years old, he could say, for this reason, "It was already then clear that God, for me at least, was one of the most certain and immediate experiences."[29]

A deeply religious phase began after the separation from Freud, when Jung, then 37, turned

---

28 "'God' is a primordial experience of man, and from the remotest times humanity has taken inconceivable pains either to portray this baffling experience, to assimilate it by means of interpretation, speculation and dogma, or else to deny it ..." 'Brother Klaus,' *Psychology and Religion: West and East*, C.W. XI, par. 480.

29 *Memories*, p. 62.

his full attention and interest to the images emerging from the unconscious. A series of numinous dreams drove him to this introspection because Freudian psychoanalysis proved insufficient to interpret them. It was a dangerous venture to descend into the realm of the unconscious having no idea where the descent would lead. Jung was in fact spared neither suffering nor terror. This phase lasted more than four years, and he found himself again and again in danger of being overwhelmed by the unconscious and its numinous contents. The unconscious encountered Jung as a *tremendum*, and in retrospect in later writings he quoted the words of Paul several times: "It is terrible to fall into the hands of the living God."[30]

Yet, looking back, Jung regarded precisely this phase of deepest introversion and introspection as particularly significant. "The years when I was pursuing my inner images were the most important in my life – in them everything essential was decided. It all began then; the later details are only supplements and clarifications of the material that burst forth from the unconscious, and at first swamped me. It was the *prima materia* for a lifetime's work."[31]

Jung was not content merely to contemplate his mystical experiences, he followed up his reflections with a rational integration of what he observed and experienced with the science of his time. He needed decades for this and the result was his life's work. Alongside this sense of intel-

---

30 Epistle to the Hebrews, 10:31.

31 *Memories*, p. 199.

lectual responsibility to his experience of the mystical or the unconscious stood an ethical responsibility that was of equal importance for him. This yielded for him, as for anyone who takes the unconscious seriously, above all the experience of the dark side of the Self, the encounter with the shadow.

In 1944, at 69 years of age, Jung fell seriously ill and, near death, had visions of overwhelming consequence. Central to these were images that displayed the *mysterium conjunctionis,* the union of opposites, in ever new and varying ways. Jung describes them in the chapter "Visions" in *Memories, Dreams, Reflections.* These were of seminal importance to scientific thought. Perhaps *Answer to Job* also originated in this experience. "I am held in thrall, almost crushed, and defend myself as best I can," Jung wrote in a letter when he was working on this book, and in another letter, "If there is such a thing as violent possession by a spirit, then this is the manner in which this book came into being." This indicates that Jung at that time grappled with an immediate religious experience, with a vision of the numinous. His deep emotionality expresses the subjection of the ego to the sovereignty of the numinous as it revealed itself to him in a dark image of God. For the sake of completeness it should be mentioned that in a later letter he commented similarly on the torment of the confrontation with that dark image of God, but then corrected his one-sidedness and added, "... at every step I felt myself contained by a blissful vision, of which I would rather not speak."

The rapturous visions were those of the *mysterium conjunctionis* that Jung had experienced in 1944 when near death. Throughout his life, dreams time and time again moved him deeply and brought him a feeling of joy. Jung was a highly gifted dreamer.

What distinguished Jung from the mystics in the usual sense of the word was that he acknowledged the epistemological limitation, thereby attributing the highest worth to the reflective and cognitive soul: "All comprehension and all that is comprehended is, in itself, psychic, and to that extent we are hopelessly cooped up in an exclusively psychic world. Nevertheless, we have good reason to suppose that behind this veil there exists the uncomprehended absolute object which affects and influences us ..."[32] If the individual is in a position to understand this and wishes to do so, "that is a confession of his subjection, his imperfection, and his dependence; but, at the same time, a testimony to his freedom to choose between truth and error."[33]

---

32 Ibid., p. 352.

33 Ibid., p. 354.

The Romantic Period in Germany*

FOREWORD

It is always risky to publish just a single chapter from a book. For this reason, I would like to indicate the context in which it is to be understood.

E.T.A. Hoffmann (1776–1829), a poet of the late Romantic period in Germany, was the author of a great many fantastic 'tales.' In the fairy tale contained in "The Golden Pot," the somewhat unrealistic youth Anselmus plays the main role. He is a typical representative of the Romantic age as his life wavers between dream and reality. He leaves his girlfriend, Veronica, in order to unite

---

* A chapter, "Die Deutsche Romantik," from the book *Bilder und Symbole aus E.T.A. Hoffmanns Märchen 'Der goldne Topf,'* by Aniela Jaffé, (Einsiedeln: Daimon Verlag, 3rd ed.,1986)

with a dream figure, the beloved little snake, Serpentina. In the end, he disappears into the fairy tale land of Atlantis. His yearning for the transcendent had completely alienated him from the world. For her part, Veronica marries a well-situated bureaucrat: thus, the split is complete.

At the center of the tale stands a mysterious golden pot, in whose shimmering surface Anselmus glimpses fabulous forms as if in a mirror. There is also a love story: the union of the beautiful fire lily with the youth Phosphorous. It is told in the manner of a gnostic myth and forms the basis for the other stories.

According to a psychological law, an extreme attitude will be compensated by a bond to the opposite extreme, or will become separated from it. Thus, an excess of collective demands was the inevitable result of Romantic one-sidedness, a longing for transcendence intensifying to the point of abandonment. How such a turn of events would affect the fate of the German people is discussed in detail in this chapter.

The numerous quotations from German Romantic literature and philosophy in the footnotes of the original German volume have been omitted with my consent. The quotations from literature contained in the text are our own translations.

A.J. in Spring, 1988

In the Romantic fairy tale, "The Golden Pot," by E.T.A. Hoffmann, Anselmus, the young hero, decides to renounce life and love in reality, and a split results between the magical and the real worlds; it is a split between consciousness and the unconscious, and characteristic of the heroes of Hoffmann's stories. Anselmus typifies all idealistic and unrealistic youths who take flight from the reality of the moment. They live entirely for their longing for the transcendent, and in the process, they elevate this yearning to a goal in itself. Such flight from the real world is genuinely Romantic, and the state of being gripped by the contents of the psychic background gives the Romantic individual his unique and characteristic imprint. This applies not only to the artists and scientists of this period, but to all the melancholy and effusive beings who called themselves "Romantics." It can be said to have always characterized the German and determined his fate. The German is the "eternal Romantic."[1] Romantic characteristics were evident even in the Middle Ages with its

---

1 Cf. Fritz Strich, *Deutsche Klassik und Romantik,* (Munich: 1928), in particular the chapter, "Europa und die deutsche Klassik und Romantik," p. 385 f. Cf. also p. 410.

mysticism and knightly ideals, and in the religious exuberance of the Baroque period, as well as in the period of *Sturm und Drang* in Germany.[2] The Romantic attitude lent its name to the 19th century, during which it reached a highpoint, and the poles of the Romantic split were driven to the extreme. Suffering from an inner cleavage which could no longer be surmounted, the era swept inexorably towards ruin, bringing down with it those individuals who had been most determined by the Romantic attitude.

Anselmus is the model of the German Romantic, the "German dreamer." He represents the German with his visionary depths and his weakness with respect to reality. In this fairy tale filled with his adventures, everything appears rather noncommittal and light. However, the images and symbols of the unconscious represent only one aspect of reality: the inner. Sooner or later, they seek their expression in the outer world. Recognition of the connection between inner and outer reality lead Heinrich Heine to his astonishing prophecy of a German revolution arising out of the developments of German philosophy and the thoughts of the Romantic period.[3] For:

> "The thought that we think ... leaves us no peace until we enable it to appear in reality. The thought will become deed, the word will become flesh. And, wonderful! the human, like

---

2 Cf. Heinrich Heine, *Sämtl. Werke,* (Leipzig: G. Fock Verlag), *Die romantische Schule* , VII, p. 127.

3 Heine, *Sämtl. Werke, Zur Geschichte der Religion und Philosophie in Deutschland,* op. cit., p. 110f., Annotation 10, p. 371.

the God of the Bible, needs only to express his thought, and the world takes form, there is light, or there is darkness; the waters withdraw from the land, or even wild beasts appear. The world is the signature of the word."[4]

Observing the thoughts expressed in the fairy tale, "The Golden Pot," from the point of view of Heine, the danger which the Romantic individual had conjured up becomes apparent.

Anselmus renounces life and withdraws to Atlantis, to the place of the primordial images, in order to remain with Serpentina, the snake, who has knowledge of the eternal truths. The Romantics typically find in life itself no meaning; they strive to understand all things in transcendental terms, and hope to fulfil their longing in death. "Death is the romanticizing principle of our life," proclaims Novalis.[5] This is the motto of the Romantic age. Everything which, in life, reminds one of death: the night, dreams, the uncanny, sickness and solitude, the supernatural and the trance, attracts them with irresistible power. Beyond the limits of life they seek its origin and its worth, and this gives life its only meaning. "Death ... (appears) as a higher revelation of life,"[6] and "Is not everything which enchants us touched by the color of night?"[7]

---

4 Ibid., p. 74. – Cf. Jung, G.W. XII, p. 322, p. 378 (C.W. XII, *Psychology and Alchemy*, pars. 394, 399, 400).

5 Novalis, *Werke und Briefe*, (Leipzig: Insel Verlag, 1942), "Fragmente," p. 331, "Blütenstaub," p. 299.

6 Ibid., "Heinrich von Ofterdingen," p. 267f.

7 Novalis, *Werke*, (Leipzig: Bölsche, Hesse & Becker Verlag), "Hymnen an die Nacht," I, p. 19.

This longing for death leads German lyrics to new heights. The "Hymns to the Night" of Novalis are truly songs of "enchantment with death," as is the following verse by Eichendorff:

"Death Rapture"

Before he sinks in the blue floodwaters
The swan still dreams and sings drunken with death;
The flowers of a summer-weary earth fade,
She lets all her fire glow in the grapes;
The sun, showering sparks as it sinks,
Gives the earth one more time glowing fire to drink,
Until, star by star, the wonderful night rises
To receive the drunken one.[8]

We are not concerned here with aesthetic or literary judgment. Also, the very real value of the German Romantic contribution in almost every field of science and art is evident. It is our aim to point out the other side of this obvious abundance: the psychological background out of which a period evolved which in turn governed the individual in conceiving his work.

A peaceful and firm rooting in this world is to the Romantic as strange an idea as the thought of living life for its own sake, and only in death to embrace the mysteries of the Beyond. Union is sought with the Infinite while still in the midst of life; or to merge with the cosmos, with the uni-

---

8 Joseph Frh. von Eichendorff, *Sämtliche Werke,* (Leipzig: 1864), I, p. 611.

verse, in order to find oneself near to God. Schleiermacher claims,

> "...that the sharply defined contour of our personality expands itself and shall gradually lose itself in the Infinite; that we, in that we become aware of the universe, also merge with it insofar as possible."[9]

But the cosmos is, in the Romantic sense, not only the universe as creation, but also the human soul. "Is then the cosmos not in us ... in us or nowhere is eternity, with its worlds, the past and the future," states Novalis.[10] Self-contemplation and contemplation of the universe are identical concepts:

> "We will understand the world when we understand ourselves, because we and the world are integrated halves. Children of God, seeds of God are we. Some day we will be what our Father is."[11]

The concept of a soul background that encompasses God and is identical with the cosmos is a legacy of ancient mystical thought.[12] However, when it no longer arises from a religious attitude but rather is erected as an intellectual edifice, it leads to dangerous arrogance and excess. "Every good man becomes more and more God. Deification, humanness, and the cultivation of oneself

---

9 Schleiermacher, *Ueber die Religion. Reden an die Gebildeten unter ihren Verächtern,* (Berlin: 1821), p. 172.

10 Novalis, *Werke,* (Leipzig: Insel Verlag, 1942), "Fragmente," p. 219.

11 Ibid., p. 406.

12 Jacob Böhme, *Das sechste Büchlein,* "Vom übersinnlichen Leben," (Amsterdam: 1682), p. 143.

are expressions that mean the same thing."[13] Or: "The highest task of formative education is to make it possible for the transcendental Self to equal the ego of the ego."[14]

Such an educational goal replaces piety with a frightening cult of the intellect and godly grace with the self-aggrandizement of the ego. The original religious goal becomes subordinated to the human will, and therein lies the germ of all lack of restraint ... "I believe in the power of the will and formative education to enable me to approach again the Infinite, to release me from the bonds of malformation, and to make me independent of the limitations of my sex."[15] The mystical experience of a connection between man and God becomes a magical means to deify the ego and elevate it to master over life and death. The ego determines their worth, whereupon life and nature are disdained and death glorified. An immediate result is the affirmation of suicide. Presented as a future ideal is the individual who, by his own will, makes himself "independent of nature;" who is able "simply by his own will to kill himself," and who will "have the ability to separate himself from his body when he sees fit."[16]

---

13 Friedrich Schlegel, *Jugendschriften*, Ed. J. Minor, (Vienna: 1882), "Fragmente," II, p. 247.

14 Novalis,*Werke*, (Leipzig: Insel Verlag, 1942), "Blütenstaub," p. 302.

15 Friedrich Schlegel, op. cit., "Idee zu einem Katechismus der Vernunft für edle Frauen," p. 268. – Cf. Schlegel, op. cit., "An Dorothea," p. 321.

16 Novalis, *Werke*, Ed. J. Minor, op. cit., "Fragmente," II, p. 193.

The scorning of earthly life as a "self-destroying illusion"[17] was a motif that the Romantics never tired of repeating. It was demanded time and time again that one should free oneself from all cumbersome earthly things. The fate of our Anselmus becomes clear when we read the words of Schubert: "All mortal striving aims toward the freeing of oneself from the bonds which tie the individual to the basis of all individuality, the earth; they hinder him from re-uniting with his eternal origin, the Cosmos."[18] The value of the earth and of life is lost. The poet Bonaventura complains: "Life flows over the individual, but so fleetingly that he calls out to it in vain to stop a moment for him and discuss with him what it wants and why it takes notice of him."[19] Everything earthly becomes a fleeting, ghostly phenomenon. Nothing is tangible any longer, for "the basis of all individuality" dissolves. Without noticing it, the individual lost in contemplation of the universe calls forth the shadow of the collective. By renouncing the earth as the basis of his special nature, he has rejected the limitations of his individuality, and so the collective soon has the upper hand; to every mad notion, gate and door are opened, and humanity is endangered. One of the first symptoms is the degeneration or loosening of control of Romantic speech. Because of their undisciplined language, exaggeration, murkiness, and immod-

---

17 Ibid., III, p. 73.

18 G. H. von Schubert, *Ahndungen einer allgemeinen Geschichte des Lebens,* (Leipzig: Reclam, 1806), 1. Teil, p. 20.

19 Bonaventura, *Nachtwachen von Bonaventura* (1805), Ed. H. Michel, (Berlin: Behrs Verlag, 1904), p. 92.

erate diction, many works of this period come across to the reader of today as exaggerated and excessive. The inexpressible shall be captured in words, but in this way, classical form disintegrates, and the standard or measure imposed upon the individual dissolves.[20]

The Romantics had lost the direct religious experience of the believing person. They were no longer mystics in the sense of the pre-occupation with God characteristic of the Middle Ages, for their consciousness was already too strong for that, too "enlightened." The 19th century knew of no mysteries that could act as a vessel to collect and contain the stream of the unconscious, that could give the experience of the godly in the human a space and a corresponding opportunity to unfold itself. When the elementary inner experiences that have moved religious individuals since time immemorial took possession of the Romantics, because they too were open to the archetypes of the collective unconscious, they were given the task of raising these images, the contents of their emotional possession, to consciousness and of understanding them psychologically. Yet, the carrying out of this task was at that time not possible, for it required a revolutionary development in psychology and the guiding line of reasoning of C.G. Jung.

His concept of the process of individuation is also, in the final analysis, a preparation for death.[21] The ability to die requires a difficult

---

20 Cf. Fritz Strich, op. cit., p. 184.

21 Cf. Jung, G.W. VIII, p. 461 f. (C.W. VIII, *The Structure and Dynamics of the Psyche,* "The Soul and Death," p. 404 ff.).

schooling and a long practice. Individuation centers around the fact that one must, in the course of life, accept death constantly as a pre-condition of inner transformation. From the standpoint of individuation, the result is very often an entirely unromantic total engagement in 'real life,' a 'dying into life', with life itself becoming the task. Inner death always means the sacrifice of a prevailing attitude toward life to a still unknown and therefore obscure new one. It means the sacrifice of the ego and its will, the ceding of this position to a greater personality supraordinate to the human being.

The Romantics could in no way protect themselves from the overwhelming power of the archetypes, neither through naive piety nor through becoming conscious psychologically. The archetypal experience became self-gratification, and aggrandizement of the ego was raised to an absolute. This striving out of and beyond oneself, the centering of life in the transcendent realm, even at that time indicated the danger inherent in the concept of the "superman," which would be proclaimed only later.[22] The counter-movement toward the outside world developed logically out of this extreme one-sidedness. Out of the originally sought-after introversion of the "folk of poets and thinkers" grew a concrete list for world conquest.[23]

---

22 In fact, the idea of the "superman" had already appeared in the work of G.F. Daumer, a Romantic scholar.

23 Thomas Mann, *Bemühungen,* (Berlin: Fischer, 1924), "Rede über Nietzsche," p. 334. – Schleiermacher, op. cit., p. 456. – Cf. F. Lion, *Romantik als deutsches Schicksal,* (Stuttgart and Hamburg, 1947).

Tragically, it is the archetype of the Self on which the Romantics foundered. They knew about a world of the ego and another of the non-ego. It was this very fact which determined their extreme emotional state and their yearning for the eternal. Clearly they intuited that the greater, impersonal, eternal world of the Self or the non-ego stands opposite that of the ego.[24] In their exuberance, however, they did not assign to the ego the role of "representing" the non-ego; of being its "symbol," and leave it at that. Rather, in reading the works of the Romantics, one gets the impression that the role of the ego was perceived as being too small and modest or even too full of suffering and arduous. They yearned for the dissolution of the ego and the cessation of earthly life in order to merge with the greatness of the non-ego, which they regarded as entirely appropriate for themselves. However, in this way man ceased to be human and finally himself appeared as a god. "Think of something finite formed in the infinite, and you think of man," or, "The human is everywhere the highest and higher than the godly," wrote Friedrich Schlegel.[25]

What Novalis called the "Non-Ego" was designated by the Romantics as the greater, eternal, primordial form of the human being. Schlegel named it "Individuality."[26] And behind the cosmos or universe so often cited by them stands the

---

24 Novalis, *Werke,* (Leipzig: Insel Verlag, 1942), "Fragmente," p. 324 .

25 Friedrich Schlegel, op. cit., "Ideen," p. 300. – Schlegel, op. cit., "An Dorothea," p. 322. – Schlegel, op. cit., cf. also p. 320.

26 Friedrich Schlegel, op. cit., "Ideen," p. 296.

image of the Great Man, the macrocosm that finds its equivalent in every individual as microcosm. This idea is found, for example, in Zacharias Werner's explanatory notes on the myth of Phosphorous or Lucifer, the primordial man. The longing of Phosphorous to be "Someone and Something," in other words, his longing for reality, for individuation, was depicted only as a liability, and the fulfilment of his longing, his life within the creation, therefore appears as an unbearable suffering. A redemption from the "prison" of life consists of a renewed dissolution, a re-immersion in the primordial "Nothing and All." Taking form in creation, true individuation, in which the ego becomes the vessel or symbol of the non-ego, the prerequisite of all consciousness, appears only as a tragic error to be remedied if possible. Werner describes it as a "delusion." One also hears this idea from Schelling: death is the "freeing of the inner life form from the outer, which holds it suppressed."[27]

Phosphorous, the "primordial human" or the "inner life form," represents, as the non-ego, the totality or the Self that, in fact, transcends consciousness, and for this reason reaches into the life-encompassing domain of the unconscious, or death.[28] If the Romantics renounce earthly existence while still in the midst of life and want to incorporate death prematurely into their lives in order to arrive at the "inner life form," they de-

---

27 Schelling, "Clara oder über den Zusammenhang der Natur mit der Geisterwelt," (Leipzig: Reclam), p. 86. – Cf. Novalis, *Werke*, (Leipzig: Insel Verlag, 1942), "Fragmente," p. 305 .

28 Cf. Ludwig Tieck, *Werke*, (Berlin: 1845), XIX, p. 267 f.

clare that the eternal side of the experience of totality alone is valid. The paradox of totality, that in order to be made real, it must be contained and made conscious out of the boundless or eternal unconscious within the boundaries of the human being, was recognized by a few of them, but the conclusions were not drawn. They only – one thinks of Novalis – surrendered to the seduction of the unconscious and death all the more intensively.

This was nowhere more clear than in their experience of love. They surmised something higher than mere earthly satisfaction, and all their songs and dramas, novels and fairy tales bear eloquent witness to their longing to grasp the secret. "Love is the ultimate goal of the history of the world, the Amen of the universe."[29] The woman is to them the mediatrix with the Beyond, she is the "last boundary of the earth."[30] Indeed, she is the universe itself that they discover in their own souls, and with which they want to become one. The beloved is "the contraction (Abbreviatur) of the universe." On the other hand, the universe appears as the "extension (Elongatur) of the loved one."[31] The relationship to the woman leads to longed-for dissolution in the universe and actually to death, where the source of life flows:

---

29 Novalis, *Werke*, Ed. J. Minor, op. cit., "Fragmente," II, p. 102.

30 J. W. Ritter, *Fragmente aus dem Nachlass eines jungen Physikers*, (Heidelberg: 1816), Fragment 483.

31 Novalis, *Werke*, (Leipzig: Insel Verlag, 1942), "Fragmente," p. 360 .

"Climb fearlessly my friend
into the well of death!
There ripples darkly
the secret source of love."[32]

Death and love became identical concepts: "Dying and loving are synonyms. In both, individuality is dissolved and death is the portal of life,"[33] writes the natural scientist Johann Wilhelm Ritter. "In death is love the sweetest, for the lover death is the wedding night, a secret sweet mystery," we read in Novalis.[34]

Alluded to here, but dealt with in more detail later, is the fact that these same thoughts underlie the images of Hoffmann's myth. The stories of the strange fates of the pairs of lovers are a single vision of the totality sought and found in love, but it is a totality that separates again and again. These images go back to the source of the mystery of life itself and reveal, perhaps, even more about the human and his mysterious relationship to love, death, life and God than the clever aphorisms and the abstract intellectual outpourings of this time.[35] Moreover, it can be said of the images of the myth that their life plays itself out in the proper place, so to speak, for it is stated that they appear in the

---

32 Friedrich Schlegel, *Werke,* (Vienna: 1846),"Weihe des Alten. An einen jungen Dichter," X, p. 29.

33 J. W. Ritter, op. cit., Fragment 629.

34 Novalis, *Werke,* (Leipzig: Insel Verlag, 1942), "Fragmente," p. 362.

35 E.T.A. Hoffmann, *Gesammelte Schriften,* (Berlin: Georg Reiner Druck und Verlag, 1871-1873), "Die Elixiere des Teufels," VI, p. 157 f., "Meister Floh," X, p. 242.

mirror of the golden pot. Thus they are enclosed in the vessel of the soul. They are like the pre-forms or preliminary stages of real life and are the structure according to which human destiny will be formed, and to which the life of Hoffmann's hero is subordinated. The myth, "The Golden Pot," is a vision of the collective unconscious; there, on the other side of consciousness, the *mysterium coniunctionis* fulfills itself as the eternal mysterious love play of the archetypal opposites. There, the Great Man appears as the luciferous messenger of God, as a light-bearer or Phosphorous. The consciously lived life, however, lies between the opposites. No love can efface the opposites, I and Thou, in life, and insight cannot delude itself when it comes to the inner conflicts. Consciousness does not prevail over the opposites in the Romantic sense, outside of life, in dissolution or in death, but rather in and through life itself.[36] The most profound symbol of humanity is the Son of God and man, Christ, who hangs on the cross of love between the two thieves, the one bound for heaven, the other condemned to hell. The paradox of the truth is valid for life and for the spirit. "Every place where a great spirit expresses its thoughts, is Golgatha."[37]

When Anselmus renounces his love for Veronica and thereby shatters the vessel of life so that he can unite "for all eternity" with the beloved snake, Serpentina, he fulfills the Romantic

---

36 Cf. Jung, G.W. VIII, p. 383 (C.W. VIII, *The Structure and Dynamics of the Psyche,* "Spirit and Life," par. 647).

37 Heinrich Heine, *Zur Geschichte der Religion und Philosophie in Deutschland,* op. cit., p. 50.

demand to release himself from the "basis of his special nature," to loose himself from the bonds of the earth. His human individuality has actually been sacrificed, and in him a mystery of love and death is also consummated. But, because he has scarcely lived and is already withdrawing from the suffering of life, a premature usurping of the totality occurs; what should only be harvested as the slowly ripened fruit of the tree of life cannot be realized outside the borders of earthly life. Anselmus sinks into Atlantis, the dreamland of the collective unconscious. Veronica reconciles herself to the bourgeois world; she also surrenders, but to the collective demands of this world, and her life accommodates itself to the narrow confines of consciousness. Two pairs, Anselmus and Serpentina, Veronica and the Privy Councillor, stand forever separated at the end, and this separation is symbolic of a latent split.

In scarcely any other piece of literature of that time is the Romantic renunciation of the limitations of earthly individuality and the resulting split into two non-individual collective worlds so impressively represented with all its consequences as in Hoffmann's fairy tale, "The Golden Pot." Hoffmann is the poet of his own time and a herald of the future. The realization or concretization of his images appeared only one hundred years later in German National Socialism, under which dominion the individual was to be submerged in the collective. The excessive collective demands to rule the world were the unavoidable result of a Romantic yearning for the transcendent raised to the point of dissolution.[38] Hitler's Germany experienced the collective death of which the Romantics sang praise, never suspecting the inexorable reality which lay behind their yearning. However, even Romantic times witnessed the first flashes of the coming storm. In 1804, Achim von Arnim, the Prussian, wrote the following "Chorus of Warriors," which one could dismiss as tasteless if it had not anticipated the malevolent spirit of the marching masses of Hitler's armies:

"We are drawn to the dark path of death,
In unbroken ranks we march;
Raging on as the tooth of one sword,
A joy to the company of many.

We hate to die the lonely death,
It is our wish to perish together,
We want to quaff happiness here,
We want to inherit bliss forever.

Let us be joyful in the night of death,
For brighter then glows life;
We have never chosen peace here,
We want to experience it in death."[39]

Equally sinister and portentous are the words of Friedrich Schlegel, which spring from the same disdain of life: "The secret sense of the sacrifice is the annihilation of the finite, because it is final," and, "In the rapture of annihilation the sense of godly creation first reveals itself. The lightning

---

38 Novalis, *Werke*, Ed. J. Minor, III, "Fragmente," p. 253.

39 Ludwig Achim von Arnim, *Ariels Offenbarungen*, Ed. J. Minor, (Weimar: 1912), p. 31.

flash of eternal life ignites itself only in the midst of death."[40]

The "rapture of annihilation" and such delusions that see in death the "sense of creation" spring from a disastrous spiritual distortion. Here, Christianity has nothing more to say and, if one prefers not to hear the voice of the Anti-Christ in such speech, then one may at least recognize in it a primitive paganism. Here speaks the spirit of Wotan, who leads the host of the dead, and who causes men to go berserk.[41]

Life is the form in which the spirit can express itself; in the final analysis, life and soul are identical concepts. For this reason, the Romantic scorn of life and praise of annihilation results in a disastrous loss of soul. In view of the experiences of our century, nothing more need be said. In this context, the words of Novalis sound like a terrible prophecy: "Collective insanity ceases to be insanity and becomes magic. Insanity according to rules and with full consciousness."[42]

In their longing for transcendence, the Romantics actually had, as Schlegel poetically put it, climbed into "the well of death" and had again uncovered the hidden spring of the German soul. But what did the dark, secret source that rippled below sing? Its song sounded strangely different from what the Romantic seekers of eternity had

---

40 Friedrich Schlegel, *Jugendschriften*, op. cit., "Fragmente," p. 303.

41 Cf. Jung, G.W. X, p. 210 (C.W. X, *Civilization in Transition*, "Wotan," par. 388).

42 Novalis, *Werke*, (Leipzig: Insel Verlag, 1942), "Fragmente," p. 342.

presumably imagined. There was nothing of peace and fulfillment, nothing of the eternal You, nothing of overcoming the world and renouncing the worldly to be heard. Rather, out of its murmuring came the wild and cruel voices of pagan gods and demons. What lies beyond consciousness is the collective unconscious. While the Romantics enthused about the collective images of the universe, the "primordial form" of the human being and an eternal embrace of love, letting themselves be swept away by these images, the ego, that laboriously achieved dominance of consciousness wrung from the primitive condition of unconsciousness, dissolved itself in inflation.[43] The old fabric of consciously created Christian culture and classical moderation received at that time a deep tear. Out of the collective soul, the spirits of the German forests appeared like triumphant messengers of a long past but as yet unforgotten time.[44]

In our fairy tale, Serpentina appears as a pagan tree spirit, and it now seems doubly fateful that this siren succeeds in drawing the hero under her spell, completely estranging him from the real world. In the beginning he could still express a slight shock at the "unchristian" name of the beloved little snake. In fact, the whole point was that he should make conscious this bit of paganism still alive in his unconscious, and by actively trying

---

43 Cf. Jung, G.W. XVI, p. 281 (C.W. XVI, "The Psychology of the Transference," par. 472).

44 Heinrich Heine, *Zur Geschichte der Religion und Philosophie in Deutschland*, op. cit., p. 57, p. 94. – Eichendorff, *Eichendorff über die Romantik*, (Munich and Berlin: A. Mayer-Pfannholz, 1925), "Die geistliche Poesie in Deutschland," p. 52.

to understand it, mature as a personality. But that would only have been possible if he had simultaneously defended and preserved his conscious standpoint and not abandoned and thoughtlessly sacrificed his Christian spirit and culture.[45]

The Germans' encounter with the primordial images of their soul represented a danger of which most had no suspicion. That danger was only recognized much later when depth psychology, particularly the theory of the archetypes and the reality of the soul, provided the necessary insight. Every individual experiences the same danger in a confrontation with the unconscious. It takes the form of an irresistible fascination with the collective contents and a compulsion to identify oneself with the archetype, instead of trying to understand it and make it conscious.[46]

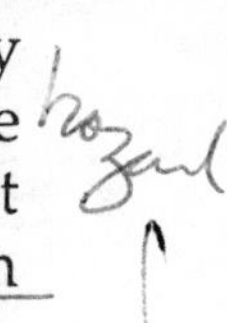

Here lies the misconception to which the Romantics fell victim. They identified themselves with the "inner man," they wanted to prematurely embody in life the "primordial form," the "eternal form in the human" or the "consummate man," and thereby achieved the opposite of what they had hoped for. They did not become gods; instead, the collective unconscious to which they sacrificed their consciousness, drowned them in

45 Georg Friedrich Daumer, *Romantische Naturphilosophie,* (Jena: 1926), p. 13 f.

46 Cf. Jung, G.W. VII, p. 76 (C.W. VII, *Two Essays on Analytical Psychology,* par. 110). – Cf. Jung, G.W. X, p. 55 (C.W. X, *Civilization in Transition,* "Mind and Earth," par. 78). – Cf. Jung, G.W. XII, p. 156 f. (C.W. XII, *Psychology and Alchemy,* par. 171 f.).

an overwhelming wave.[47] At the end of their era, which had begun so exuberantly, only a small group of suffering or broken beings remained. More than one was destroyed by death or insanity, and had to suffer the disintegration of the ego as the bitter fulfillment of his longing for the transcendent.[48] Instead of the future ideal of a "new human" came a regression into a primitive German pagan world.

The Romantics were scarcely capable of realizing that, in their disdain for the human individual and the limitation of his earthly existence, they had smoothed the way for a depersonalized mass for which nothing else remained but to seek its *Führer*. Even at that time, Heinrich Heine had written in connection with the *Kyffhäusersage* the strange prophecy of a man awaited by the German *Volk* who would reign with "a loud voice" and with the "crossless crown of an emperor;" a man to rule without Christianity, in other words.[49]

The Romantic age was a century in which the unconscious was especially powerful. Such periods in the life of the individual and in the life of a nation are a time of inner change and transformation. Contents arise from the unconscious which could enrich and renew the worn out con-

---

47 Friedrich Schlegel, *Jugendschriften*, op. cit., "Fragmente," p. 291. – Novalis, *Werke*, (Leipzig: Insel Verlag, 1942), "Fragmente," p. 303.

48 K. Hilfiker, *Die schizophrene Ich-Auflösung im All*. – Cf. E.T.A. Hoffmann, *Schriften*, op. cit., "Prinzessin Brambilla," X, p. 193.

49 Heinrich Heine, *Sämtl. Werke*, (Leipzig: G. Fock Verlag), "Elementargeister", VIII, p. 109 f.

scious attitude. The first century in our reckoning of time was also such a period, and it bore the fruit of Christianity. In Christianity, as at that time in other religions, in the cult of Mithra and in the Egyptian religion, the honored Son of God or God-incarnate found its deepest and most beautiful expression.

The two millennia which followed are the history of the interaction of the human being with this image of God. In the Reformation and in philosophy, a transformation occurred in the image of God and a gradual fading set in. Heinrich Heine, in his inspired discourse, "On the History of Religion and Philosophy in Germany," forecast the death of the Judeo-Christian god and mourned this event in advance.[50] The sensitive artistic nature of the painter Philipp Otto Runge felt lost in a time which he described in a letter: "... among us ... something is lost; we stand at the edge of all religions which have grown out of Catholicism ... Everything seeks something definite in this uncertainty and doesn't know where to begin."[51] Jean Paul had a vision of the end of the world which moved him to the depths, later worked out in his novel, *Siebenkäs*, under the title, "Discourse of the Dead Christ delivered from the Top of the World Building, contending that there is no God."[52] A century later, C.G. Jung, on the basis of his observation of unconscious processes,

---

50 Heinrich Heine, *Zur Geschichte der Religion und Philosophie in Deutschland,* op. cit., p. 72 f.

51 Philipp Otto Runge, *Briefe,* (Berlin: 1913), p. 110.

52 Jean Paul, *Siebenkäs,* (Leipzig and Vienna: Bibliogr. Institut), p. 193 f.

could ascertain a "time of the death and disappearance of God."[53] Out of the recognition of the archetype and its inner dynamism, he sets forth the consequences of such a death of God, or rather, of such a transformation of God.

The image of the death of God is a typical experience of the soul. It expresses the idea that the highest, life-granting, sense-giving value has been lost. "This death or loss must repeat itself again and again: Christ always dies, as he will always be reborn, for the psychic life of the archetype is timeless in comparison to our individual boundedness by time."[54] The highest worth is apparently destroyed; still, it will arise again renewed, if perhaps in a changed way. With regard to the latter, there seems to be a singular consensus in the unconscious of numerous individuals; it is the precondition of its effectiveness. Jung recognized this new form, in which the highest value rises again out of the unconscious: "The place of the deity appears to be taken by the wholeness of the human."[55] This wholeness must not be confused with the ego personality. It pertains much more to the "inner being," to what the Romantics had also encountered as the "primordial form," or as "Phosphorus." But they could not explain this archetype, let alone consciously endure the tension implied by such an experience. Like Anselmus,

53 C.G. Jung, G.W. XI, p. 98 (C.W. XI, *Psychology and Religion*, par. 149).

54 Ibid. – Cf. also G.H. v. Schubert, *Ahndungen einer allgemeinen Geschichte des Lebens*, op. cit., 2.Teil, I, p. 410.

55 Jung, G.W. XI, p. 89 (C.W. XI, *Psychology and Religion*, par. 139).

they could not maintain the tension between the ego and the archetypal world. As early as then, the development had already begun that finally led to the psychological insight of Jung, who recognized in the Self the pre-existing, greater personality of the God-incarnate embracing both consciousness and unconscious. This, above all, showed modern man on his path towards consciousness the way of individuation, a new and internalized possibility for realizing the *Imitatio Christi.*[56] This is the spiritual way of the individual, and the *Imitatio Christi* stands outside the confessions.

The transformation of the Christian concept of God as an archetypal event of death, descent into hell, and resurrection forms the background of all the historical events from whose horror and apparent senselessness the world suffers. In following Jung's interpretation, one recognizes not only a meaning, but more than this, a way out of the hellish confusion. For this reason, the following brief and meaningful sentences are now presented:

> "I only know – and here I am expressing what countless other people know – that the present is a time of God's death and disappearance. The myth says he was not to be found where his body was laid. 'Body' means the outward, visible form, the erstwhile but ephemeral setting for the highest value. The myth further says that the value rose again in a miraculous manner, transformed. It appears as a miracle, for when a value disappears, it always seems to

56 Jung, G.W. XII, p. 21 f. (C.W. XII, *Psychology and Alchemy*, par. 7).

be lost irretrievably. So it is quite unexpected that it should come back. The three days' descent into hell during death describes the sinking of the vanished value into the unconscious, where, by conquering the power of darkness, it establishes a new order, and then rises up to heaven again, that is, attains supreme clarity of consciousness. The fact that only a few people see the Risen One means that no small difficulties stand in the way of finding and recognizing the transformed value."[57]

There is nothing more to add to these words, except to conclude briefly by summarizing what has been said up until now. The difficulty for Hoffmann, as well as for his Romantic contemporaries, lay in the fact that they confronted in the images of the soul religious contents, upon which they no longer knew how to impose order. They no longer possessed, for example, the naïvety of the alchemists, who in their chemical/philosophical train of thinking belonged to a pagan religion, while nevertheless conceiving of themselves as good Christians; nor were the Romantics able to understand the psyche as the origin of religious phenomena. They took as metaphor all those who, up until the time of Romanticism, occupied themselves with inner images, primarily the alchemists and the mystics. These images bore witness to God or to a godly mystery, while modern psychology, on the basis of these same images, attempted to understand the nature of the

---

57 Jung, G.W. XI, p. 98 f. (C.W. XI, *Psychology and Religion*, par. 149).

psyche. The Romantics stand, so to speak, on the threshold between mysticism and psychology. Everything in them tended toward understanding and making conscious the experiences which led them over the borders of consciousness and filled them with ecstasy and paroxysms of mystical possession. *That they could not do so at that time was their fate, and they were marked to a greater degree than any other generation, by the tragedy of transition.* Behind this transition looms a transformation of the image of God.

The fate of the fairy tale hero, Anselmus, in "The Golden Pot" is not merely the fantastic creation of a poet, but the typical expression of an era: "Every work of art has a personal and a collective origin; it is an expression of an individual and the expression of a time."[58]

---

[58] Aniela Jaffé, *Bilder und Symbole,* op. cit., p. 7.

The Individuation of Mankind

In 1955 the Federal Institute of Technology (E.T.H.) in Zürich awarded C.G. Jung, then 80 years old, an honorary doctorate in the natural sciences. Among other things acknowledged in the *Laudatio* was: "the interpretation ... of the individuation of mankind."

Jung had never used this expression in his writing; he himself spoke of mankind's becoming conscious, or, as in the "Epilogue" to *Psychology and Alchemy*, of the drama of an *Aurora Consurgens* that began in prehistoric times and extends through the ages into the distant future.

It is characteristic of Jung that he represented this drama of development, this collective individuation, as a religious-psychological event, for as far as he was concerned the central theme of the development was the gradual transformation and unfolding of the image of God. The idea of an interaction between the dawning of consciousness in mankind and the transformation of the God image occupied him for decades, and he sought constantly to formulate it in new ways.

Nevertheless, his being honored as an interpreter of the individuation of mankind was based upon a generalization. In working out his conception of a collective individuation, Jung had occupied himself almost exclusively with the transformation of the Judeo-Christian image of God. This implied no value judgement, as from his psychological standpoint all religions are archetypal picture- and word-images with their own validity. Yet it was the Judeo-Christian God image that most directly concerned Jung. His interpretation of its collective development contained some of his most profound but also most difficult ideas.[1] It is therefore essential to explain at the outset what he understood by 'God,' what by 'God image,' and, finally, what 'individuation' meant to him.

Although it was his aim to support his statements scientifically, psychologically or historically, his ideas can only be fully understood if they are also seen as very personal expressions arising from a genuine and deeply religious attitude. God was for Jung "the absolutely unfathomable,"[2] but at the same time, "one of the most certain immediate experiences."[3] When he was 84 years old he

---

1 Jung expressed his views on this theme above all in "A Psychological Approach to the Dogma of Trinity," in C.W. XI. – *Aion*, C.W. IX, ii. "Answer to Job," C.W. XI. – "Epilogue" to *Psychology and Alchemy*, C.W. XII.

2 *Letters, I,* (June 12, 1933 Maag).

3 *Memories,* p. 62.

affirmed that his *raison d'être* lay "in the confrontation with the undefinable being that man calls 'God.'"[4] These words already indicate a major difficulty in Jung's psychology of religion, which lies precisely in the fact that God can neither be defined nor investigated. And the nature of the so-called 'collective unconscious,' that sphere which transcends consciousness and the world, is just as undefinable and unknowable as the nature of what is called God.

When Jung spoke of an 'experience of God,' he meant an experience of an incomprehensible force that operates autonomously and unpredictably in the psyche, in life and in nature like a foreign will, a power of fate before which the human being feels subordinate and powerless.[5] Jung himself was to have many such 'experiences of God,' which began when he was a child.

Autonomous power and incomprehensibility also characterize the effects arising out of the collective unconscious. It is the archetypes which from a consciousness-transcending sphere preform our dreams and fantasies, lie at the root of our inspirations and fears, and decisively influence our body, behavior and our fate. Faced with the power of the archetypes, the ego-will retreats

---

4 *Letters, II,* (Mar 13, 1958 unnamed addressee).

5 Cf. *Die Beziehungen zwischen dem Ich und dem Unbewussten,* G.W. VII, p. 261 ("The Relationship between the Ego and the Unconscious," in C.W. VII, par. 400): "When, therefore, we make use of the concept of a God we are simply formulating a definite psychological fact, namely the independence and sovereignty of certain psychic contents which express themselves by their power to thwart our will, to obsess our consciousness and to influence our moods and actions."

into the background. Only one thing can be determined regarding the origin of the autonomous and irrational effects to which man and life are exposed: they derive from a sphere that cannot be comprehended. Psychologists call it 'the unconscious,' the religious person calls it 'God.'

Jung himself, as he explained in *Memories, Dreams, Reflections*,[6] preferred the term 'the unconscious,' presumably knowing that he could just as well speak of 'God' if he wished to express himself mythically; and whenever he used the word 'God,' then he was always aware that it was synonymous with the unconscious.

This synonymity or indistinguishability between God and the unconscious did not remain a merely theoretical idea, but also played a role in Jung's psychotherapy. Jung always sought to clear the individual's path to an experience of the numinous. According to one of his letters, he would say to a person tormented with irrational fear, "Well, do not try to escape this fear which God has given you, but try to endure it to the end - *sine poena nulla gratia* (without punishment, no grace). I can say this because I believe I am a religious man and because I know with scientific certainty that my patient has not invented his fear, but rather, that it is preordained. By whom or by what? By *the Unknown.* The religious individual calls this 'the hidden God,' the scientific intellect calls it the unconscious."[7]

It appears to be a contradiction at first when Jung, despite describing the unknown at certain

---

6 *Memories, p.* 336.

7 *Letters, I,* (Dec 10, 1945 Buri).

times as God and at other times as the unconscious, nevertheless rejected the idea that these two concepts were identical. He wrote, "It is by no means certain that what is designated as the unconscious is so to speak identical with God, or set in the place of God." Yet the indistinguishability of God and the unconscious derives from the fact that the unconscious "(is) the medium from which, for us, the religious experience appears to spring."[8] Only by means of the psyche can the individual relate to a metaphysical reality. For this reason the religious mystery seems to be grounded in the psyche itself.

For the faithful, religions are revelations of the godhead itself, and the individual believes that he truly expresses God when he says the word 'God.' For psychology as an empirical science, the origin of religions and dogmas lies in the human psyche. That is to say, what was originally undefinable takes on definition in image or word within the conscious mind. "One must always remember that God is a mystery, and everything we say about it is said and believed by human beings. We conceive images and concepts, and when I speak of God I always mean the image man has made of Him. But no one knows what He is like unless he is a god himself."[9] The Catholic theologian Karl Rahner formulates the idea in a similar way: "Whoever does not love the mystery, does not know God; he continuously looks past Him, the proper and true God, and worships not Him

---

8 *Gegenwart und Zukunft*, G.W. X, p. 523 ("The Undiscovered Self (Present and Future)," C.W. X, p. 245 ff.).

9 *Letters, II,* (Aug 17.57 unnamed addressee). *Letters, II,* (Aug 17, 1957 Roswitha N.).

but the image of Him made to our specifications."[10]

Images of God are made by humans, write both Jung and Rahner. More precisely, images of God are rooted in experiences of the human being. He experiences them intuitively or says they are revealed to him; or else they come to him amid his pious reflections on the mystery of life and the creation. The formulation, the 'making' of the image of God, is nevertheless removed to a great extent from his will or his intellect. For man is free neither in his gnosis nor his contemplation. Both, along with revelation, are shaped by factors in the unconscious: the archetypes. Underlying the image of God is a form-giving central archetype, unrecognizable as such but which manifests itself as a concrete image in the consciousness.

Here, too, it is impossible to distinguish between psychological and religious concepts. Just as the godhead is indistinguishable from the unconscious, the images representing God are not distinguishable empirically from images symbolizing human wholeness, the symbolism of the Self. Jung interpreted his dream, in which a diamond-like star high above mirrored itself in a pool, with the words: "The *imago Dei* (Image of God) in the darkness of the earth, that is myself."[11] The star is the image of God and is the image of the Self. They possess mirror-image similarity, and when St. Paul spoke of "Christ in me," (Gal. 2:20) the image of the Son of God became for him a symbol

---

10 Karl Rahner, *Schriften*, VII, p. 505. – Cf. Jung, *Letters, II,* (Oct 1, 1953 Niederer).

11 *Letters, II,* (Dec 18, 1946 White).

of the Self.[12] Jung noted a great number of dreams in which the old revered symbols of God, such as the circle, the cross, the great mother, the almighty Father, light and the Trinity, can be interpreted as images of human wholeness. The individual experiences the image of God as reality in his own psyche and, for this reason, the old wisdom that self-knowledge paves the way to knowledge of God has retained its validity.

Jung never tired of emphasizing that he was only concerned with the investigation of the archetypal *images* of, and human statements about, God. Their structure and characteristics interested him. He regarded them as psychic facts which he observed from an empirical standpoint. The individual is not at all in a position to say anything about God himself or the metaphysical concept of God since, according to Jung: "Truly we are confronted with frightful enigmas."[13]

A careful reading of Jung's letters and his works on the psychology of religion nevertheless shows that he is not always consistent in maintaining an empirical attitude. This is presumably not possible because 'archetype' and 'archetypal' are already borderline concepts. The word 'archetype' comes from *typos:* a blow or imprint. It thus presumes an act of imprinting.[14] But by

12 Cf. G.W. XII, p. 33 f. (*Psychology and Alchemy,* C.W. XII, par. 22), "The 'Christ symbol' is of the greatest importance for psychology in so far as it is perhaps the most highly developed and differentiated symbol of the self, apart from the figure of Buddha."

13 *Letters, II,* (Oct 1, 1953 Niederer).

14 Cf. G.W. XII, p. 28 (*Psychology and Alchemy,* C.W. XII, par. 15).

whom? "We simply do not know the ultimate derivation of the archetype," wrote Jung.[15] And he added, "It would be a blasphemy to assert that God can manifest himself everywhere but in the human soul."[16] In other words, God reveals himself in the psyche as an archetypal image of the godhead, and with this assertion Jung comes very close to a metaphysical statement. Jung expressed the same thought in a rejoinder to an attack by Martin Buber,[17] who accused him of psychologism: "God has indeed made an inconceivably sublime and mysteriously contradictory image of himself, without the help of man, and implanted it in man's unconscious as an archetype, an archetypal light: not in order that theologians of all times and places should be at one another's throats, but in order that the unpresumptuous man might glimpse an image in the stillness of his soul that is akin to him and is wrought of his own psychic substance. This image contains everything he will ever imagine concerning his gods or concerning his psyche." Jung led up to these sentences with the words, "Here, just for once, and as as exception, I shall indulge in transcendental speculation and even in 'poetry'..." In the final analysis, Jung had to let the matter rest with the indistinguishability of God and Self. When he was 80, he wrote: "It is unfortunately true: (the human) has and holds a mystery in his hands and at the same time is con-

15 Ibid., (par. 15).

16 Ibid., p. 23 (par. 11).

17 G.W. XI, p. 661 f. (Religion and Psychology: A Reply to Martin Buber," in *The Symbolic Life*, C.W. XVIII, p. 663 ff.).

tained in his mystery. What can he proclaim? Himself or God? Or neither? The truth is that he doesn't know who he is talking of, God or himself."[18]

Jung never understood the reference to the synonymity of the godhead and the unconscious, or the synonymity of the archetype of the godhead and the archetype of the Self, to be a reduction of God to a merely psychic factor, as he was often accused of doing. "I do not by any means dispute the existence of a metaphysical God," he wrote to a critic, "I permit myself, however, to put human statements under the microscope."[19] And at another point: "I don't overlook God's fearful greatness, but I should consider myself a coward and immoral if I allowed myself to be deterred from asking questions."[20] Scarcely a scientist before Jung had ventured to lend the psyche such a significance. Through the archetype of the godhead, the psyche is endowed with an inherent creative religiosity, and thus it partakes of "limitless range and unfathomable depths."[21]

Godhead and unconscious are synonymous concepts. The symbols of the Self cannot be distinguished from symbols of God. These are two fundamental psychological assertions. At times, the godhead is portrayed as something unknowable, and at other times, it is symbolized by well-

---

18 *Letters, II,* (May 23, 1955 Amstutz).

19 Ibid., (May 5, 1952 Buri).

20 Ibid., (Apr 30, 1952 White).

21 G.W. XII, p. 27 *(Psychology and Alchemy,* C.W. XII, par. 14).

defined contents. In the history of religion, these apparently contradictory facts correspond to myths of God as an Ineffable and an Unfathomable that nevertheless is validly portrayed through sacred images and symbols.

Among the Cabbalists, too, one finds the concept of a formless hidden deity that reposes invisible in the depths of its own being. But alongside this, and just as valid, is the concept of an outwardly manifesting godhead of mystical form that reveals itself in images and names.[22] "The godly is not only the formless abyss in which all is engulfed, although it is that too; it contains in its outward orientation the guarantee of form," writes Gershom Scholem.[23]

It is somewhat surprising to note that the hidden element in Zohar, significantly portrayed as 'En-Sof', must not be translated as "He who is Endless," but rather as "That which is Endless." By means of the use of the neuter form, mystic Jewish thought avoids any personal nuance and any visualization. Similarly, in another text, the hidden God is termed "That which is Unfathomable," not "He who is Unfathomable."[24] The sacred symbols and names of God as form are looked upon as His 'mystical robe.' In a mysterious way, the formless substance of the godhead is nevertheless immediately present in the

---

22 Cf. Gershom Scholem, *Von der mystischen Gestalt der Gottheit*, (Zürich: 1962), p. 30 ff. and *Die jüdische Mystik in ihren Hauptströmungen*, 1957, in particular p. 11 ff.

23 Gershom Scholem, *Von der mystischen Gestalt der Gottheit*, p. 34.

24 Gershom Scholem, *Die Jüdische Mystik in ihren Hauptströmungen*, p. 13.

symbolic form of God, and "The truer the form, the more powerful the life of the formless element in it."[25] Jung's religious-psychological formulations are related to the dualistic image of God described in Cabbalistic mysticism. There exists a parallel between the hidden, unknowable, mystical godhead, En-Sof, on the one hand, and the unconscious on the other. The unconscious, being synonymous with the godhead, is also hidden and ineffable, and the psyche belongs in its totality "to the darkest and most secret that our experience encounters."[26] The unconscious is also 'endless,' for its boundaries cannot be specified.

The Cabbalistic symbol of the 'mystical robe of the godhead,' that is to say, its manifold images and representations, corresponds to the archetypal symbols that refer to the Self, which cannot be distinguished from symbols of God. For, according to Cabbalistic tradition, the hidden 'infinite' is contained in its entire reality in these images of the godhead. In the same way, the archetype of the Self unites limited consciousness with the boundless unconscious. It is temporal and eternal, unique and infinitely various.

The analogy between the religious ideas of Jewish mysticism that developed hundreds of years ago and modern psychological scientific knowledge can be explained only through the archetypal structure of the psyche. Images and thoughts expressing the mysteries of being are structured by archetypes, the timeless patterns in

---

25 Gershom Scholem, *Von der mystischen Gestalt der Gottheit*, p. 34.

26 G.W. XII, p. 18 (*Psychology and Alchemy*, C.W.XII, par. 2).

the unconscious. In his contemplation man is also shaped by them. In their religious genius the Jewish mystics intuitively grasped the essence and limits of metaphysical concepts and expressed them in paradoxical religious images and ideas. It is likewise significant that the scientific attitude of the psychologist Jung contains a genuine, even passionate, religiosity. In the final analysis, the one cannot be separated from the other.

Finally, it should be pointed out that the concept of God held by the Protestant theologian Paul Tillich sounds similarly dualistic.[27] Behind all religious and confessionally defined forms of God stands a "God above God," indefinable and absolute. He is "the unending source of all that is holy," and shines throughout the forms of the historical religions, although he may never be identified with them; for that would be an inadmissable limitation of the indefinable, infinite nature of God.

To conclude my previous remarks, I would like to add a word about the concept of individuation. It means simply that anything created develops into its own form and fulfills its own destiny; in other words, that its Self or its Idea manifests itself. Yet this unfolding must always be understood as just approaching that pre-existent totality; not, however, as its complete realization.

Jung related this process of development not only to human beings, but also to animals, plants and inorganic nature. A transcendent creative principle, an Idea, a Self, reveals itself even in

---

27 Paul Tillich, *Auf der Grenze*, 1962, p. 166, and *Der Mut zum Sein*, 1965, p. 185.

these.[28] In general, the process is natural and unconscious in humans as well. Nevertheless, man is the only creature given the possibility of a conscious individuation, that is, the possibility of recognizing at least in part those forces which underlie his own being, thinking, behavior and development, as well as the apparently random whims of fate. Such a recognition adds an inner dimension to life. Outer and inner realities inseparably comprise a whole. Both are aspects of the Self that unfold just as much in outer events and physical existence, in destiny and in character, as in the inner psychic world, in dreams, fantasies, visions and moods. These structures of the unconscious provide the meaning-giving complement to the processes of outer life, and through them individuation unfolds in successive stages.

Yet, we should not forget that the archetype of the Self realizing itself in existence is not distinguishable from the archetype of the godhead. From this point of view, one cannot avoid seeing individuation as an unfolding of the 'godly.' The conscious experience of life becomes a religious experience: one could also say that it becomes the fulfillment of a godly mission.

Jung wrote to a nineteen year old youth, using, as he liked to do, the language of myth: "One must be able to suffer God ... my inner principle is: *God and man.* God needs man in order to become conscious, as He needs limitation in time and space. Let us therefore be for Him that limitation in time and space, an earthly tabernacle."[29]

---

28 Cf. *Letters, II,* (Aug 3, 1953 unnamed addressee).

29 *Letters, I,* (Apr 30, 1929 Corti).

In the relationship between God and man or the Self and man, a decisive role falls to the infinitely smaller one of the two, the human being. For in order to emerge from the concealment of the unconscious and be recognized, and in order to realize itself in individuation, the archetype requires man, or consciousness. However, the archetype's tremendous impulse to unfold stands in the way of this necessary limitation in time and space. As its becoming conscious through the minds of individual men can only ever succeed in a fragmentary way and as the transcendent never completely fulfills itself in limitation, the unfolding process continues without end. It continues throughout the history of mankind, insofar as this is the history and development of a discriminating consciousness.

The history of mankind is accompanied by changing myths and images of God, just as, in the case of individuals, outer events are accompanied by inner images. In them, the mighty archetype of the godhead renders itself visible in ever new aspects, although never in its totality. The development of the image of God, and the history of consciousness which perceives this development and transforms in accordance with it, are two sides of the same process, which the *Laudatio* honoring Jung designated as the "individuation of mankind."

Even in early times the transformation of the image of God led to the idea of an 'evolving God.'[30] Jung did not reject the idea of a god in the

---

30 Cf. Ernst Benz, *Theologie und Wandlung des Menschen bei F. W. J. Schelling*, Eranos 23-1954, p. 305 ff.

process of evolution in the sense of a metaphysical statement. Still, he sought to complement this idea with the psychological interpretation of a corresponding development of consciousness: "If we describe God as evolving, we must bear in mind at the same time that He is perhaps so vast that the process of cognition only moves along His contours, as it were, so that the attribute 'evolving' applies more to it than to Him."[31]

The setting side by side of the metaphysical and psychological views only alluded to here is characteristic of Jung's reflections on religious statements. He was aware that it was impossible "to state with certainty whether these changes affect only the images and concepts of God, or concern the ineffable itself."[32]

For the reader, especially for the theologian, this is no small problem. On the other hand, it lends to the thoughts and analyses of Jung the great scope which characterizes his work; and it is impressive that he repeatedly called himself back to order and empirical facts so as to provide empirical evidence for his intuition of the metaphysical; one could say, to anchor his visions in the historical realm.

At the center of the Jungian interpretation of a collective individuation stand three processes of development: the transformation from the Old Testament to the New Testament image of God, the unfolding of the trinitarian image of God and indications of a transformation into a quaternarian image of God, as well as the event desig-

---

31 *Letters, II,* (May 23, 1955 Amstutz).

32 Cf. G.W. XI, p. 388 ("Answer to Job," C.W. XI, par. 555).

nated by him as the "continuing incarnation," which will be the main topic of discussion here.

Freud also posed the question of the transformation of the Old Testament into the New Testament God, and in his late work, *Moses and Monotheism,* gives an answer.[33] According to Freud, Moses was a high-ranking Egyptian who pledged the children of Israel to the original monotheism of Egypt and led them out of bondage. Nevertheless, Moses, later their idol patriarch, was murdered by them,[34] which evoked a growing, although unconscious, feeling of guilt in the Jewish people. This burden of guilt finally gave rise to the idea of atonement, according to which a son of God lets himself be killed although he is free of sin, thereby taking upon himself the sins of all. "It had to be a son, for it had been a murder of the father." Later this idea of atonement would be understood as a message of redemption and would be hailed by St. Paul as Gospel. With this, the old God the Father stepped behind Christ. "Christ the Son took the the place of God just as every son had longed to do since time immemorial." And in another passage: "It is an appealing supposition that the remorse surrounding the murder of Moses provided the impulse for the fantasy of a Messiah who should come again to bring his people redemption and world dominion as promised. If Moses were the first Messiah, then Christ is his restitution and his successor." And, "(Christ was) the returning an-

33 Freud, C.W., XVI.

34 Freud refers here to the work by E. Sellin, *Mose und seine Bedeutung für die israelitisch-jüdische Religionsgeschichte,* 1922.

cestral father of the primitive tribe transfigured, and as son set in the place of the father." Jung saw the transition from Judaism to Christianity in another connection, which I will try to illustrate. There exists between Jung and Freud a strange agreement: both see a dark, evil, immoral deed as leading to the transformation. Freud saw the evil as being in the human being and he placed the origin of the transformation in the murder of Moses by the children of Israel. Jung saw the evil in a sphere that transcended the human and placed the origin of the transformation in the wager of God with Satan, which was intended to test the loyalty of the pious Job.

The transformation of the Judeo-Christian image of God comprises the main content of Jung's much-discussed book, *Answer to Job.* Jung regarded the statements of the Holy Scriptures as utterances of men; that is, as formulations of archetypal contents, which is why his interpretation of the Book of Job also remains in the realm of psychological images. But because a pre-existent, unconscious and therefore ineffable reality forms the basis for the archetypal images, we can, in the final analysis, never know "how clear or unclear these (religious) images, metaphors and concepts are with respect to their transcendental object."[35]

The deep emotion out of which *Answer to Job* was written leaves no doubt that Jung's interpretations concern not only images and concepts, but also lay before us a religious affirmation, a truly moving confrontation with the Ineffable. But it is

---

35 G.W. XI, p. 388 ("Answer to Job," C.W. XI, par. 555).

one which will again and again be verified through the psychological interpretation of the biblical text. He completely ignored modern theological explanations. For him, the sole concern was the mythological-archetypal substance of the religious statements. He was concerned with what was generally believed at the time and its psychological background.

In view of the mysterious proceedings in the Book of Job, the question also arises as to whether the intellect is in the end the best and the only instrument suited to their understanding, or, if it is not experience which leads us closer to an approximate understanding.[36] Paul Tillich once wrote: "All discussion of godly things is senseless if it does not occur in a state of deep emotion."[37] Jung himself was deeply moved by the content of the biblical book of Job. It was for him a paradigm for an experience of God not only as a benevolent-creative entity, but also as an equally terrible and destructive autonomous power, an experience that has retained its validity, in our time more than ever before.

He was moved in a similar way by the terrific revelations of God in the apocalyptic vision of St. John. He discussed these in the second half of *Answer to Job.* Through Jung's critical interpretation of the God-image of the Apocalypse, the occasional accusation that his critique of the God-image in the Book of Job is an expression of anti-

---

36 Cf. G.W. XII, p. 549 f. *(Psychology and Alchemy,* C.W. XII, p. 483).

37 Tillich, *Works,* VIII, p. 118.

semitism can be proved untenable.[38] He himself complained bitterly that most of his readers stopped reading in the middle of *Answer to Job.*

It was Jung's emotional tone which irritated his readers and still irritates them today: his anger at the inscrutable dark power against which he cried out in harsh and, as he admitted, often unjust words. There were only a few who followed him and understood him in this experience. One was Henri Corbin, and this touched Jung deeply. In his detailed, almost hymnal article about the book, he recognized Jung as someone who experienced and who suffered.[39] "It is because we are here in the presence of a man *alone* that I would like to invite all those who feel isolated to reflect upon this book, to listen to this message, if they are truly *alone* ... This theology is not learned in books or by historical critique of writings, but in the night and in the suffering of the soul, in the sublime inner battle fought without compromise, or cowardice, or abdication."

In a letter dated December 5, 1951,[40] Erich Neumann wrote to Jung regarding *Answer to Job:* "It is a book that moved me deeply. I find it the most beautiful and profound of your books, whereby I mean to say that it is actually not a 'book' any more. In a certain sense, it is an argu-

38 To emphasize the negative side of the Judaic image of God in Hebrew Literature cf. the quotation in *Aion,* G.W. IX, 2, p. 68 (C.W. IX, par. 106), which Zwi Werblowsky, Jerusalem, had prepared for Jung.

39 Henri Corbin, "La Sophia éternelle," in *La Revue de Culture Européenne* III, 5, Paris 1953. (Corbin was Professor for Islamic Religions at the Sorbonne.)

40 Cf. *Letters, II,* Erich Neumann to Jung, (May 12, 1951), p. 243.

ment with God, an entreaty similar to Abraham's when he remonstrated with God because of the fall of Sodom. It is, for me personally, an entreaty against a god who let six million people be slaughtered, for Job is precisely Israel. I don't mean that in the 'narrow' sense; I know full well that we are only the paradigm for all of mankind, in whose name you speak, protest and comfort. And exactly the deliberate one-sidedness, yes, the frequent incorrectness of what you say, is for me an inner proof of the necessity and righteousness of your attack - which actually is no attack at all, as I well know."

The experience of the negative aspect of God and the vehement debate with God was for Jung only the starting point for his reflections. In the end he sought to understand, "Why and to what purpose Job was wounded, and what consequences have grown out of this for Yahweh as well as for man."[41] With these words he alluded to thoughts on the development and transformation of the image of God.

'God and man' is the great theme in the drama of the Book of Job, and what is unprecedented is the fact that a man is spoken of who, in spite of all trials imposed upon him, shows himself to be superior to God. He was superior with respect to morals, for God's afflictions were not justified and struck no transgressor of the law, but an humble and pious man. He was superior to God also in the decisive matter of consciousness. As Omniscient, God should have known the man

41 G.W. XI, p. 394 ("Answer to Job," C.W. XI, par. 563).

Job from the beginning; still, He let Himself be seduced by Satan into doubts regarding him and into the gruesome playing out of His wager. He behaved as if He were unconscious. Job, on the other hand, recognized God, and thus he could speak the words: "I have heard of thee by the hearing of the ear: But now mine eye seeth thee" (Job 42:5).

Jung saw it as decisive that Job, in all his guiltless misery, does not lose his faith in the totality that is God. Instead he is even certain that, in the end, he will find in this very God a helper and an advocate against God. "As certain as he is of the evil in Yahweh, he is equally certain of the good."[42] He had become conscious of the antinomy in the godhead, and this had to lead to a transformation. "This is what happens in Job: *The Creator sees Himself through the eyes of man's consciousness, and this is the reason why God had to become man.*"[43]

From the point of view of psychology the story of Job involves the encounter of a man with the image of God or the image of the Self, whose "devastating reality"[44] confronted him from the outside, as in a projection. Job's recognition of the contradictory aspects of God demonstrates a superiority of consciousness with respect to the Self or of man with respect to God. A new interpretation of the archetype, a new myth was thus required, in which the image of God would also

---

42 Ibid., p. 396 (par. 567).

43 *Letters, II,* (May 3, 1958 Kelsey).

44 Cf. G.W. XI, p. 660 ("A Reply to Martin Buber," C.W. XI, p. 663 ff.).

carry characteristics of the superior man. Thus, the way to a new level in the individuation of mankind was prepared.

The transformation in the relationship between man and the image of God, or consciousness and Self, derives from the balance of a constantly altering energy potential between these two inseparably bound entities. At times, the archetype of the Self powerfully forces itself into the consciousness and, by means of its dynamism, causes its transformation and expansion; at other times consciousness undergoes change and penetrates, by means of the strength of its cognitive capability, deeper into the former unconscious. In both cases, the individual transforms and the image of totality also transforms. Yet it can never be decided with certainty which preceded and what resulted. In the case of Job, one should not exclude the possibility that the process originated in the Self's impulse to unfold; that, in the religious language used by Jung, God sought out the encounter with the man Job out of a mysterious longing for recognition and realization.

The myth of the Son of man or God-incarnate that now emerged unfolded slowly over a period of centuries. Jung subjected the biblical report of this transition to a careful psychological analysis.[45] I can only indicate here that the first signs of the transformation are recognizable, for example, in Ezekiel's vision of the human figure on the heavenly throne (1:26, 2:1) and in Daniel's vision of the Ancient of Days (7:13).

45 Cf. Jung's detailed description in "Answer to Job," G.W. XI, p. 452 ff. (C.W. XI, p. 421 ff.).

The decisive transformation first appeared, however, with the New Testament message that God became incarnated in Jesus and took the limitations and suffering of man upon himself. In this myth of the incarnation of God, that is, in God's life and death as Son of man and God-incarnate in the form of Christ, Jung saw the answer to Job: the acknowledgement of his consciousness and superiority as man, as well as of the injustice that God had done him.

Jung ascribed to the role of Christ in this myth a divine transformation of far greater significance than the role of the man Jesus and his probable life story, which today is often placed in the foreground by theologians. Jung fought to prevent the reinterpretation or elimination of the mythical elements in the Gospel, just as he, in general, criticized any attempt to de-mythologize. He held this to be the cause of an irreplaceable and, for the soul, dangerous loss.

Naturally, he formed for himself a personal picture of the man Jesus: "I am, as a matter of fact, so profoundly impressed by the superiority of this extraordinary personality ..."[46] and he saw in the miracle-working wandering rabbi Jesus a man in the mode of the ancient Jewish prophets : he compared him to John the Baptist or, also, to the much later Zaddikim of Hasidism. But neither the character nor the life of Jesus suffice to explain "one of the most astounding intellectual and religious effects of all times," which began with him. The agent of the drama lay much more in the mighty workings of pre-existing archetypal

46 *Letters, II,* (Nov 24, 1952 Sinclair and Jan 7, 1955 Sinclair).

motifs, especially in the tiding of the God-incarnate, which had been constellated since Job and corresponded to the spirit of that age. The idea of an incarnation of God in Christ developed "out of the collision of an extraordinary personality with a very special *Zeitgeist.*" Jung did not deny that the adaptation process of Jesus' humanness to the transcendent and nonhuman figure of a divinity remains in the final analysis an impenetrable mystery. To the American author Upton Sinclair, he wrote: "Sure enough, we must believe in reason. But it should not prevent us from recognizing a mystery when we meet one. It seems to me that no rational biography could explain one of the most 'irrational' effects ever observed in the history of mankind."[47]

From a psychological standpoint, the "incarnation of God" is a symbol of individuation in man: in the process of individuation, the archetype of the Self, which is synonymous with the archetype of God, seeks to actualize itself. Thus the individuation of man and the incarnation of the Divine in man are one and the same event expressed in different languages and from two different perspectives. Seen from the perspective of the individual or of consciousness, it is called individuation; seen from the dynamic of the archetypal image of God, it is called incarnation. And because the individuation process of the individual continues in the individuation of mankind, this, too, can be understood as a progressive incarnation of the Divine. This will now be the subject of discussion. Jung spoke in this connec-

---

47 Ibid., (Nov 3, 1952 Sinclair).

tion not of the individuation of mankind, but rather of "the real history of the world." Literally, "The real history of the world seems to be the progressive incarnation of the Deity."[48]

A biblical prefiguration of the intimate connection between God and man is found in Genesis in the words expressing an image of likeness: God created man in his own image. The goal of the individuation of mankind appears to lie in the realization of this tremendous fact, a goal that is, to be sure, just as unattainable as the full realization of the pre-existing Self in the individuation of the single individual. Also, in the individual's process of becoming conscious, the Self retains its paramount magnitude in relation to the human being, and the godhead loses nothing of its original boundless totality through the incarnation.[49]

In contrast to Jung, Freud understood the attainment of consciousness as a finite process: "Where the 'Id' was, the 'Ego' shall be," according to him,[50] and nothing characterizes more impressively the difference in the way the two masters viewed the world.

According to Jung's conception, the incarnation of God is not yet completed with the incarnation in Christ, for Christ was no earthly being according to the religious mythology. He was conceived of the Holy Ghost, and Mary, his mother, was free of original sin. Christ stood more on the divine than on the human side, and he remained

---

48 Ibid., (May 3, 1958 Kelsey).

49 Ibid., (Jan 2, 1957 unnamed addressee).

50 Freud, Ges. Werke XIII, p. 285.

without sin.[51] It was, so to speak, God's good side that had incarnated itself in Him - Job's advocate against the God who had put him to the test.

Being identical with God's light side, Christ became the mediator and redeemer of man, and proclaimed a benevolent and loving God. The Judaic image, containing within itself the contradictory aspects of a god who was as just as He was unjust, gave way in the gospel of Christ to the idea of an unequivocally good God. Jung presumed that this unequivocal decision for the goodness of God (Mark 10:8, Matthew 19:17) was found unsatisfactory by the conservative Jews because, with respect to their image of an ambivalent God, this signified a limitation.[52]

Even Jesus was still aware of God's dark side, otherwise He would not have taught His disciples to pray that God should not lead them into temptation, a situation in which He himself had been placed. Nor would St. John have left behind his revelation of a dreadful outbreak of horror in future generations without such a premonition of evil. In the same way, it appears an almost incomprehensible tragedy that the man Jesus taught of a benevolent God, but Himself had to die a gruesome death in order to reconcile this

51 Cf. "Answer to Job," G.W. XI, p. 460 ff. (C.W. XI, par. 690). Jesus repulsed the temptation of the devil (Mark 1:12, Luke 4:1) and with this separated his shadow from himself. The fact that the dark side of Jesus was also reported in the New Testament (cursing of the fig tree, Mark 11:12 ff., attitude toward the mother, John 2:4, the taking of another's she-ass, Matthew 21:2) could not hinder the interpretation by the church fathers of Christ as equal to the benevolent God proclaimed by him.

52 *Aion*, G.W. IX, 2, p. 68 (C.W. IX, par. 105).

God with man; a fact that, because of the proclamation of the oneness of God and his Son, also permits a completely different interpretation.

Despite a lingering sense of the dark side of the Creator, the image of God underwent a splendid development in the course of the first centuries after the birth of Christ culminating in an image of highest spirituality, the Trinity. God became the Supreme Good and the darkness of the original image of God remained absent. But because the dark side, or what is designated as evil, remained a reality, it too was able to find mythical expression. It became embodied in the figure of God's adversary, the devil.

The devil carries on the tradition of the Old Testament Satan. Whereas Satan had been counted as one of the sons of God who were regarded as "elements of the Godly substance and surrounded God as a 'heavenly assembly',"[53] the devil was cast out from God's presence. Jung interpreted the strange words of Jesus (Luke 10:34) in terms of this banishment or separation: "I beheld Satan as lightning fall from heaven." The banishment from the heavenly realm, the fall to earth, announced, according to Jung, the dominion of the devil as lord of the material and earthly world. He now stands in diametric opposition to the loving side of God in heaven and is understood as the negation of the spiritual and good; and thus, as the negation of all that represents the essence of Christ. It was as if the opposites latent in the image of God had fallen asunder.

---

53 Cf. R. Schärf, *Die Gestalt des Satan im Alten Testament* in Jung, *Symbolik des Geistes*, see p. 253.

From a psychological standpoint, that process of splitting, that opposition of Christ and devil, fulfilled the archetypal pattern of the hostile brothers which had already found expression in Horus and Seth, Ormudz and Ahriman, Cain and Abel, and Esau and Jacob. Among the early Judeo-Christians in the time after Christ the idea of the two sons of God developed, of which the elder was called Satanael, and the younger, Christus.[54] According to the Homilies of Clement, Christ was God's right hand and the devil God's left. The natural and unconscious tendency of the soul to find equilibrium and symmetry is expressed in these and similar images; therefore a *Summum Bonum* (supreme good) must be compensated by an *Infimum Malum* (infinite evil).

In the patriarchal world of Judaism, the individual is still directly sheltered by a law that encompasses the spiritual and the earthly in a single divine order. This order is anchored deep in the essence of the Biblical-Judaic religious attitude, which is based on a sanctification of life as a whole.[55] For this reason the Mischna, the collection of religious laws in the Talmud, states that the individual shall serve God with his good and his bad "inclinations," including all his vital energies and sexuality.

For the Christian, another ethical norm is valid: if he is secure in his belief and in the Church, he seeks to emulate Christ as a model of the good

54 Michael Psellus, *De Daemonibus*, 1497.

55 Cf. Zwi Werblowsky, "Das Gewissen in jüdischer Sicht," in *Das Gewissen*, Studien aus dem C.G. Jung-Institut Zürich, 1958, particularly p. 104 f.

and spiritual. One could say : the Christian believer serves God with his good "inclinations." But because the vital or instinctive drives had found no place in religious observance, these sank into the unconscious and were bound to that content which Jung designated as the shadow of the personality. This shadow is not only comprised of everyday human wickedness and error, but, in the broadest sense, represents a compensatory reality to the culture canon of any given time.

Light and darkness are inextricably part of humanness and life. From the perspective of Jungian psychology, the shadow will never be subdued or eradicated; but the individual does have the opportunity to hold its negative effects in check through consciousness of his actions. If the shadow remains unconscious, the individual is far more apt to be at its mercy and can easily become the tool of evil. It is well known that perfectionists are often exactly those most disturbed or thwarted by negative forces from the unconscious. Freud pointed out the neurosis-inducing effect of an exaggerated adaptation to the dictates of the culture canon, or Super-Ego. The 2000-year history of the Christian era shows that Christianity, despite its message of love and the teaching of a benevolent God, could not hinder the tragedy of historical development, which in our century threatens to lead to catastrophe. Man has not matched the achievement of a tremendously expanded knowledge of the outer world with anywhere near the equivalent knowledge of his own inner nature, especially the shadow. For this reason, man was not in a position to resist the dark and driving forces repeatedly breaking out of the unconscious, and the intellect also became an instrument of destruction.

This is the historical and moral situation, in the context of which Jung's psychology of religion can best be understood. He was aware that he was not addressing those individuals who were secure within their religious belief, and that is also true today. The faithful do not require any exposition of the Scriptures with respect to their archetypal background and their psychological significance. Jung addressed those who can no longer believe but wish to know and understand, because they are affected by the plight of their time or because they are seekers. And that holds true for individuals of all confessions, and for layman as well as clergy.

It was a childhood trauma for the ten-year-old Jung when he overheard his father, the minister Paul Jung, imploring God in a desperate prayer to give him the ability to believe. Jung attempted to provide an answer to such a predicament. In this, he was not concerned with the pronouncement of a new doctrine or truth, but with a new symbolic or psychological understanding of holy texts and dogmas. Jung wanted to show how closely the old religious statements relate to the individual himself, and that he will experience this if he has the courage to confront the numinous archetypal images in his psyche. In the process of becoming conscious, the individual experiences the image of God as a reality in his own soul. In this context it is significant that the confrontation with the shadow is one of the first tests of courage upon submerging oneself in the unconscious.

Freud had already confronted man with his shadow.[56] But Jung also saw the religious connection. Psychologically, the shadow represents the dark aspect of the Self that also seeks to realize itself in individuation. In mythological or religious terms, the shadow signifies the dark side of the image of God lacking in the Christian concept. Understood from this point of view the realization of the shadow amounts to a change in the relationship between the godhead and man. In a way, it is as if God, following the incarnation of His light side in Christ, would now incarnate His light side *and* His darkness. In doing so, this more complete incarnation would not be realized in the form of a single divine son, but rather in His ordinary earthly creature, man. "The guilty man is eminently suitable and is therefore chosen to become the vessel for the continuing incarnation, not the guiltless ... for in him the dark God would find no room,"[57] according to Jung. In other words: the dark side of God only finds space where the individual is conscious of the darkness which works in him and recognizes it as an essential and functioning part of his personality. With such a consciousness, or with the more complete incarnation, the way is prepared for a new stage in the individuation of mankind.

The realization of the 'partial incarnation' of which the Christian myth speaks is related to the psychological fact that the archetype, on account of its boundlessness, can never be accepted com-

---

56 Cf. *Letters, II,* (Dec 27, 1958 Hull).

57 "Answer to Job," G.W. XI, p. 494 (C.W. XI, par. 746).

pletely by consciousness, but only in a continuously flowing process. In addition to this, a powerful inertial force opposes the impulse to transformation and attaining consciousness. The same is true in individual life: the one who makes an effort to become conscious will be confronted with this retarding and inhibiting tendency in the unconscious. "The unconscious wants to flow into consciousness in order to reach the light, but at the same time it continually thwarts itself, because it would rather remain unconscious." And that means in a figurative or religious sense: "God wants to become man, but not quite."[58]

With the more complete incarnation of the godhead, that is, with the more complete image of God or a totality which includes both light and darkness, the message of Christianity is in no way invalidated. In most cases, making the shadow conscious amounts to a deep emotional shock. For this reason, it can only be recognized and accepted without ill effect when sufficient light has previously been made conscious. The feeling for one's own worth must not be lost, and the darkness must not prevail. The "incarnation of the good" must already have taken place, so that the individual is capable of taking a stand against the evil which is part of him and his life without falling victim to it. It requires virtue and wisdom "... to assimilate the dark God who also wants to become man, and at the same time endure him without perishing."[59]

---

58 Ibid., p. 490 (par. 740).

59 Ibid., p. 491 (par. 742).

Conscious individuation makes new ethical demands on the individual: one could speak of a renewed transformation of the ethical norm.[60] He will be confronted with good and dark forces of the Self while the one as well as the other seeks to materialize itself. For this reason, difficult and painful situations can ensue, in which adaptation to the cultural canon and rejection of it seem to be demanded with equal insistence. The individual will be called on to make a decision between obedience and disobedience. Good and evil lose their sharply defined contours. Out of this uncertainty grow conflicts of conscience and collisions of duty, according to Jung, "the loneliest thing ever dreamed of by the loneliest of all, the Creator of the world."[61] Nevertheless, he saw an ethical value in the decision that results from such an inner conflict, this state of "supreme doubt," and he regarded it "as not particularly meritorious morally for a person to avoid everything that is customarily considered a sin."[62]

He himself experienced such a collision of duties when he left Freud. Lengthy inner battles preceded his decision, which he made in obedience to his inner voice, but in so doing disobeying the recognized norms of filial affection, loyalty, respect and gratitude. Seen from the point of view of the cultural canon, he followed his shadow. His suffering and loss of direction in the period fol-

---

60 Cf. Erich Neumann, *Tiefenpsychologie und Neue Ethik,* (Zürich: 1948), *Depth Psychology and a new Ethic,* new English edition in preparation.

61 *Letters, II,* (Jan 13, 1949 Fierz).

62 Ibid., p. 521.

lowing the separation from Freud are indicative of how difficult the decision was for him.

Conflicts of duty demand of the individual a high degree of consciousness. Jung saw them as "milestones of individuation," for "Without thorough knowledge of 'good and evil,' ego and shadow, there is no recognition of the Self."[63] In suffering ethical conflicts, the Self mirrors itself in its opposites; in Jung's mythical language, "... the 'oppositeness' of God has taken possession of him..."[64] Jung saw a symbol of this difficult experience of the totality in the central Christian event: in Jesus, the man, suspended on the cross between the two thieves, the one good, the other evil, the one destined for heaven, the other for hell. That such a daring interpretation of the Crucifixion met with resistance is understandable.

From a psychological standpoint, the criterion for the ethical attitude of the individual is consciousness of his own deeds. For this reason, Jung wished to have Christ's words as an ethical motto: "Man, if indeed thou knowest what thou doest, thou art blessed; but if thou knowest not, thou art cursed, and a transgressor of the law."[65] Jesus said this to a man whom He saw working on the Sabbath.

Naturally, consciousness may never be abused as a freedom to do evil out of subjective whim, for "Even on the highest peak we shall

---

63 *Letters, II,* (Feb 16, 1954 Kirsch).

64 "Answer to Job," G.W. XI, p. 447 (C.W. XI, par. 659).

65 *Codex Bezae,* apocryphal insertion at Luke 6:4.

never be 'beyond good and evil' ... for, as in the past, so in the future the wrong we have done, thought or intended will wreak its vengeance on our souls, no matter whether we turn the world upside down or not."[66]

Job too had experienced the contradictory nature of Yahweh, but he still experienced the godhead as an infinite Other, which confronted him from without as an inexplicable power of fate. The conscious individual also recognizes that his image resides as an unfathomable antinomy in his own deepest nature[67] and, as such, has worked through him since time immemorial, as history shows.

The individual who has experienced the light and the darkness and become conscious of them as realities of the Self can understand the gospel of love and the benevolent God as only a part of the truth. The godhead appears to him more as a *tremendum,* before which the Old Testament reaction of fear of God is still a valid one. "It is terrible to fall into the hands of the living God," is stated in the Epistle to the Hebrews (10:31) and in the revelation of St. John (14:6), an angel announces the "eternal Evangelium," whose content above all evokes the fear that is God's due. Jung indicated this when he wrote in *Answer to Job,* "Man can love God and must fear Him." Only an image uniting both aspects of the godhead would overcome the dualism inherent in the Christian

---

66 "A Psychological Approach to the Trinity," G.W. XI, p. 196 (C.W. XI, par. 267).

67 Cf. G.W. XII, p. 33 ff. (*Psychology and Alchemy,* C.W. XII, p. 29 ff.).

religion, a dualism that, though denied, has existed until now. Thus, the idea of a redemption of the devil gains a new meaning, a meaning which Origenes articulated as early as the second century after the birth of Christ but which was never supported by the church.

Within Judaism, the image of God that included good and evil achieved differentiated form in the Cabbala.[68]

In the course of Christianity's intellectual history a few outstanding individuals, like Nicolas of Cusa and Jakob Böhme, have also professed their belief in a God both good and evil.

For Jung's psychology of religion, it was of decisive significance when he came upon numinous images of the union of rationally incomprehensible opposites in the fantasies and speculations of the alchemists. Yet they were not concerned with the moralistically formulated opposition of Heaven and earth as good and evil, but rather with the value-free antinomy of spirituality and materiality.

In the experiments of the alchemists, Mercury not only plays a role as quicksilver, but also represents an incarnated Word (Logos), a *Deus Terrenus;* and the philosopher's stone was not only mineral, but also spiritual. It was regarded as a redeemer and was named "The Savior of the Macrocosmos." The gold they sought was at one and the same time metal and a philosophical or

---

68 Cf. Gershom Scholem, "Gut und Böse in der Kabbala," in *Von der mystischen Gestalt der Gottheit,* op. cit., p. 49 ff.

religious idea, an image of God; in addition, it was said that it worked with equal effect both as a poison and as a healing and protective medium.

Not only was the spirit sacred to the alchemists: material was also sanctified, and they never regarded it as either hostile to the spirit or as something to be overcome.

For this reason the fantasies of the alchemists are revealing from a psychological standpoint, because as images close to dreams they grant a glimpse into those unconscious processes accompanying consciousness which are often preparing its transformation. In other words, the unconscious proves itself to be a more or less modifying partner of consciousness. In the images of the alchemists one can thus recognize an unconscious tendency to compensate the spiritual emphasis of Christianity with nature and the material world. The central forms and images of the alchemists are new symbols of the Self spontaneously created by the psyche. They attempt to bridge the split in the Christian view of the world, the split between spirit and material or spirit and nature, with a compensatory paradox.

The role that the feminine plays in the symbolism of the alchemists points in the same direction. The alchemical wedding counts as a high point of the *opus.* In this *mysterium conjunctionis* the opposites in the form of the masculine and feminine amalgamate in a union which for the alchemists represented the much sought after 'treasure.' The characteristics of immortality and eternity attributed to it indicate that here too the creation of an image of God is involved.

Henri Corbin placed Jung's interpretation of the Old Testament Sophia, the Wisdom of God, in the heart of his essay, *Answer to Job.* Corbin considered Jung's ideas regarding her transformation and movement towards the Christian trinitarian image of God as so significant that he gave his essay the title, "The Eternal Sophia," and expressed his belief that Jung would one day be seen as the "prophet of the eternal Sophia."

According to Jung, this image of the eternal feminine emerges during the history of the Christian religion in ever changing forms: As the mother of God, as the sun-woman of the Apocalypse, and finally as Mary, whose Assumption in dogma was proclaimed in 1950. In this transformation of the image of the feminine he also saw the process of a collective individuation.[69]

Jung sought to illuminate the collective individuation process from many different sides, describing it in terms of the transformation of various symbols. The symbol of the eternal feminine shows such a transformation, as does the development of the trinitarian image of God toward a quaternarian image of totality. The progressive incarnation, with which we have primarily been concerned here, represents a further line of transformation.

The development of consciousness proceeds according to a regular pattern in that all these sequences of symbols finally culminate in an image of totality which unites the opposing factors. In the process of the continuing incarnation,

---

69 Cf. Erich Neumann, *The Great Mother,* (Princeton, 1955), p. 325 ff.).

positive and negative, creative and destructive forces unite to form a paradoxical image of God. In the complementary experience, these same forces appear in the consciousness of man as opposites within his wholeness - as his own inner reality.

The dogma of the bodily assumption of Mary is also a symbol for a union of opposites, for the feminine is moved into proximity with the masculine heavenly Trinity. Throughout history the feminine has symbolized nature, the corporeal, and the material, in other words, all those factors which are lacking in the Christian spiritual image of God. The feminine is now taken up into the metaphysical realm, as emphasized by the physical assumption of Mary.

This metaphysical spanning of the opposites of masculine and feminine principles, of spirit and nature, appeared so meaningful to Jung that he attributed the utmost importance to the Assumption of the Virgin Mary.[70] An allusion to that symbolic union of opposites is found in the official commentary as the image of a *hierosgamos*, which states that Mary united with Christ in the heavenly bridal chamber.

Viewed historically, the veneration of Mary, a tradition reaching far back in time, formed the basis of the new dogma. In psychological terms, it can be understood as an expression of a union of opposites which had already been present in the

70 A transformation of the trinitarian into a quaternarian image of God did not take place, for Mary was not elevated to goddess, but rather remained *deipara* (God-bearer or set-equal-to-God). The way to such a transformation has at best only been prepared.

unconscious for quite some time, and had fired the imagination of the alchemists of the 16th and 17th centuries.

Any discussion of a collective individuation is a discussion about the spirit of an age. It is significant that interest surrounding the 'union of opposites' in the image of God or with respect to human wholeness is by no means confined to religion and psychology. The physicist Wolfgang Pauli held "the imagined goal of overcoming of opposites ... for the articulated or unarticulated myth of our own time."[71] And the poet Gottfried Benn also declared "The fusion of Everything with the opposite concept" as "the spiritual hallmark of our epoch."[72]

Today one knows that the unity of our world would disintegrate without the creative tension of its opposites, and this insight is mirrored everywhere in the thinking of our time: there is no doubt that, in the act of cognition, subjectivity and objectivity coincide. In the life of the psyche, a death drive complements the pleasure principle. The individuation of mankind is rooted in the tension between consciousness and unconsciousness, between the inner world and the outer world. Eastern and Western religions and philosophies appear ever more clearly as aspects of *one* spirit. Finally, the trend toward recognizing instinct and spirituality, or more specifically, sexuality and

71 Quotation after W. Heisenberg, "Wolfgang Paulis Philosophische Auffassungen" in *Ztschr. für Parapsychologie und Grenzgebiete der Psychologie III*, Nr. 2/3, 1960, p. 127.

72 Quotation after H. E. Holthusen, *Der Unbehauste Mensch*, 1964, p. 35.

spirituality, as inseparable aspects of the totality is another example.

For centuries the church had proscribed the forces of sexuality with the result that, in our century, a conspicuous countermovement set in. This, in its turn, led to an exaggerated emphasis on sexuality; sexuality became, so to speak, fashionable. Recently, the necessity of a reconciliation of religious spirituality and sexuality has been discussed even in ecclesiastical circles, though in the face of great opposition. The possibility of marriage for priests has become an issue, and this discussion, as well as the numerous publications on this subject[73] indicate a possible trend toward a more unified view.

We are indebted to Freud for redeeming sexuality from its taboo status. However, his ideas were not based on a conception of sexuality and spirituality as opposites: he saw the spirit as derivative of instinct and the result of its sublimation.

Jung rejected the concept of sublimation, for he regarded the spirituality in man as an instinct in its own right while acknowledging a spirituality in sexuality. "But my main concern has been to investigate, over and above its personal significance and biological function, its spiritual aspect and its numinous meaning, and thus to explain what Freud was so fascinated by but unable to grasp."[74]

---

73 Here are named only: Walter Schubart, *Religion und Eros*, 1941; Stephan Pfürtner, *Kirche und Sexualität*, 1972; Wolfgang Trillhaas, *Sexualethik*, 1970.

74 *Memories*, p. 168.

Sexuality is an expression of the earthly spirit, the dark side of the Self or image of God that Jung also called "the other face of God."[75] Sexuality as such cannot be spiritualized; it remains what it is, namely nature; but nature, Jung recognized, which is within the framework of religious totality. In this sense, the tension between the opposites dissolves in a polarized unity, as an expression of eros beyond time and space.

The overcoming of the opposites is the myth of our time, as Pauli wrote. Nevertheless, to expect that the striving for unity or the attempt to unite opposites could serve to ward off once and for all the dangers threatening our culture would be an illusion. The significance of these efforts toward a union of opposites lies much more in the fact that they represent alternatives to the one-sidedness of consciousness and rational thinking, for it was this one-sidedness which led to the spiritual, social and political split within the world. The efforts toward a union of opposites have a compensatory character, and one could thus view them as the beginnings of a new transformation.

With this I would like to return to my starting point and summarize once again: through conscious individuation or continuing incarnation the human being is, so to speak, participating in the unfolding of the image of God: the process of transformation of the image of God corresponds to mankind's process of becoming conscious.

"Man is the mirror which God holds up to himself, or the sense organ with which he apprehends his

75 Ibid.

being," according to Jung.[76] In psychological translation, the Self is revealed in the human act of reflection.

To be sure, the impulse driving this evolution appears to originate in the transcendent archetype; nevertheless, human consciousness is needed to recognize the antinomy and experience this polarity as its inner reality. At a subsequent stage, human consciousness is once again required to recognize the opposites into which the archetype or the God-image had split, in order to restore this union. "The *mysterium conjunctionis* is the business of man,"[77] wrote Jung to Erich Neumann, continuing even more drastically, "God is a contradiction in terms, therefore he needs man in order to be made One ... God is an ailment man has to cure."[78]

It was important for Jung to find the same thought in the Cabbala of Isaak Luria (1534-1572): that the human being is to employ the forces he has to participate in and aid the divine life process, that the human is, in fact, indispensable in the work of redeeming the world, and that this redemption lies in uniting the opposites within the godhead.[79] As, according to Luria, the vessels which, in the course of the mysterious act of world creation, God made to receive the divine light, proved too weak and cracked, everything that has since existed has been left with an inherent flaw;

---

76 *Letters, II,* (Mar 28, 1953 Amstutz).

77 Ibid., (Jan 5, 1952 Neumann).

78 Ibid.

79 Cf. G. Scholem, *Die jüdische Mystik in ihren Hauptströmungen,* 1957, p. 267, "Isaak Luria und seine Schule."

all things and all humans to a certain extent carry the crack within themselves. The secret goal of all development lies in the restoration of the primordial condition before the crack occurred, that is, in a process which can be conceived of as a "perfecting of God." This restitution of all things to their true state requires "not only an impulse that originates in God, but also an impulse originating in the man which he created," for the human participates in the divine cosmic event, when, in prayer and in every action, he makes it his inner objective to restore the original unity and "unify the name of God."

Jung saw great superiority in the thoughts expressed in the Lurian Cabbala: "The Jew has the advantage of having long since anticipated the development of consciousness in his spiritual history. By this I mean the Lurianic stage of the Cabbala, the breaking of the vessels and man's help in restoring them. Here the thought emerges for the first time that man must help God to repair the damage wrought by the Creation. For the first time man's cosmic responsibility is acknowledged."[80]

If one compares Jung's interpretation of the individuation of mankind with Teilhard de Chardin's representation of a development of humanity,[81] two very different goals can be seen. For Teilhard de Chardin the goal lies in a perfecting of the human being and in the harmony of a unified humanity; and he believed in its realiza-

---

80 *Letters, II,* (Feb 16, 1954 Kirsch).

81 Cf. Teilhard de Chardin, *Der Mensch im Kosmos,* 1959. – A. Portmann, *Der Pfeil des Humanen,* 1960.

tion after an almost unimaginable period of more than one million years.

Seen from the standpoint of Jung's psychology, the shadow of man excludes his perfection from the outset.The goal lies much more in achieving the highest degree of consciousness, whereby the recognition of an inner world with its light and its darkness compensates for extraverted knowledge of the world. To the same extent that human consciousness deepens, the archetype of the Self or godhead can unfold and the individuation of mankind proceed. When and if this unfolding or individuation ever comes to an end is a question that cannot be answered. Still, one may suppose that the dynamic of the boundless autonomous archetype drives the development on for as long as there is a consciousness to respond.

Jung's interpretation of an individuation of mankind is no analysis of history. Nor does it correspond to any exact chronology, for the stages of individuation overlap one another. Rather, it was an attempt to uncover the inner aspect of a development of consciousness spanning thousands of years and to trace the autonomous archetypal transformation which accompanied it. The older Jung became, the more important this inner history appeared to him. A few months before his death he wrote: "It is quite possible that we look at the world from the wrong side and that we might find the right answer by changing our point of view and looking at it from the other side, i.e., not from outside, but from inside."[82]

---

82 *Letters, II,* (Aug 10, 1960 Earl of Sandwich).

As a psychotherapist, Jung was, above all, concerned with showing the individual a way to an experience of the psyche that could also be understood as religious. It is then that the religious accounts and dogma reveal their truth in a new light and the individual is placed in the midst of the process of revelation. In Master Eckhart's words: "If I were not, then God were also not; that God is God, of this I am a cause – if I were not, then God were not God." And he added: "It is not necessary for this to be understood."[83]

Jung knew that a descent into the depths of the psyche also must be understood as a myth, for the experience of the psyche borders on the unknowable, and the individual, in his perception of that which transcends consciousness, is also determined by the archetype. Jung's greatness appears to me to lie in the fact that, despite all the erudition and care that went into his scientific interpretation, he left the mystery untouched. He felt himself just as duty-bound to the human as he was to the unfathomable. The words with which I would like to close also testify to this: "No one can know what the ultimate things are. We must therefore take them as we experience them. And if such experience helps to make life healthier, more beautiful, more complete and more satisfactory to yourself and to those you love, you may safely say: 'This was the grace of God.'"[84]

---

83 Predigt über Matthäus.

84 G.W. XI, p. 117 (*Psychology and Religion*, C.W. XI, par. 167).

Transcendence

Following the essay on individuation, a few remarks might be in order about Jung's attitude toward the matter of life after death, a subject that has occupied mankind since time immemorial. The heightened interest today is probably to be understood as a symptom of fear in a threatened world: certainty is sought in an uncertain situation. Thus over the last decades a wide-ranging literature has evolved addressing the age-old human questions about karma and reincarnation, as well as experiences of dying and of the hereafter.[1]

Jung, too, wrote on this subject.[2] He addressed himself again and again to the question of wheth-

---

1 An interpretation of experiences of death from a Jungian point of view by L. Frey-Rohn, "Sterbeerfahrungen psychologisch beleuchtet" in: v. Franz, Frey-Rohn, Jaffé, *Im Umkreis des Todes,* (Zürich: Daimon Verlag, 1980), p. 27-97. English edition in preparation.

2 Jung, G.W. VIII, p. 461 ff. (C.W. VIII, *The Structure and Dynamics of the Psyche,* "The Soul and Death," p. 404 ff.) – "On Life after Death," in *Memories,* p. 299 ff.– Jung, *Letters, I* and *II.*

er a recognition of events or conditions in the sphere beyond earthly life, that is, in the realm of the transcendent, was at all possible for man. Jung never doubted the fact that nature and life, cosmos and psyche, border on a "mysterious sphere," on something unfathomable. "We must face the fact that our world with its time, space and causality relates to another order of things lying behind or beneath it, in which neither 'here nor there' nor 'earlier nor later' are essential concepts."[3]

Jung's views are confirmed and taken further by analogous findings in the natural sciences. To give just one example, the Swiss biologist Adolf Portmann also referred to a "non-dimensional sphere" beyond empirical – physical and psychic – reality.[4]

There are parapsychological phenomena, for example, extra-sensory perceptions, prophetic dreams, premonitions, etc., which indicate that the soul reaches at least partly into that transcendent sphere, that "it shares in a form of being which is outside time and space, and therefore is not subject to change and transformation."[5] It

---

3 Jung, *Memories*, p. 305. – Cf. G.W. XIV/2, p. 332 (C.W. XIV, *Mysterium Conjunctionis*, par. 787): "That the world inside and outside ourselves rests on a transcendental background is as certain as our own existence."

4 Regarding the recognition of a transcendental reality on the part of the natural sciences, cf. A. Jaffé, "The Hidden Reality," in *The Myth of Meaning in the Work of C.G. Jung*, (Zürich: Daimon Verlag, 3. Edit., 1986), p. 29 ff.

5 Cf. "Seele und Tod," G.W. VIII, p. 475 ff.("The Soul and Death," in C.W. VIII, *The Structure and Dynamics of the*

possesses, according to Jung, "a partly eternal quality." And out of that ensues not the certainty, but presumably the possibility of a continuation of life after death, which nevertheless cannot be imagined in concrete terms. It remains a mystery. Characteristic of Jung's thinking and a sign of his intellectual integrity is the fact that he let the mystery endure. He was constantly aware that everything which transcends the world and life, the so-called hereafter or a metaphysical reality, in the end remains unknowable to man: "*The world beyond conscious comprehension is a reality,* an experiental fact. We simply cannot understand it."[6] This acknowledgement of epistemological limitation was fundamental to Jung's scientific approach.[7]

Knowledge of a transcendent realm is denied us, because all of our understanding and all of our experience depends on our psyche, and we "are bound by our whole being and thinking to this world."[8] Thus, everything which is known only appears to be identical to what is yet to be known. In reality, only that which the psyche experiences as an impression or image of what is to be perceived can be perceived . "We can in imagination and belief go beyond the psyche, just as in fantasy we can go beyond the three-dimensional world. But

---

Psyche, p. 404 ff.). – Cf. Jaffé, "Der Tod in der Sicht von C.G. Jung," in *Im Umkreis des Todes,* op. cit., p. 11-29.

6 *Letters, II,* (May 3, 1958 Kelsey). Jung's italics.

7 Cf. G.W. XIV/2, p. 324 ff. ("The Self and the Bounds of Knowledge," in C.W. XIV, *Mysterium Conjunctionis,* p. 544 ff.).

8 *Memories,* p. 300.

we can have immediate *knowledge* only of the psychic."[9]

It is nevertheless characteristic of the nature of man, that he cannot be content with these limitations. Or better, he is conscious of them only in rare cases. He is a seeker, and his spirit wants answers to the questions with which life and death confront him.

Jung speaks of the "mythical man" living in every one of us; he is the one who "demands to transcend the limits." Out of his own spiritual source, he creates images and myths which variously represent or symbolically portray the unknowable. And yet, he never consciously thinks out or invents these images. They are contents arising out of the collective unconscious which in dreams, visions or fantasies become visible and recognizable as images, and which move him deeply. They are not objective statements about the transcendent, yet they are "real" as effective expressions of the psyche.[10]

For Jung, the subjectivity of these images and myths was a scientifically necessary observation and did not imply an inferior valuation. In the same sense the fact that the unconscious is an incomprehensible entity does not imply an inferior valuation of dreams. Quite the contrary: "I lend

---

9 *Letters, II,* (Feb 12, 1959 Tanner). – Cf. J. Jeans, physicist, "The true object of scientific research can never be the reality of nature, merely our observation of nature," *Physik und Philosophie,* 1952.

10 Cf. M.L. von Franz, *Traum und Tod,* (Munich: Kösel Verlag, 1984). *On Dreams and Death,* (Boston: Shambhala, 1986).

the strange myths of the soul an attentive ear," Jung wrote in *Memories, Dreams, Reflections.*[11]

Man, especially the aging person, follows an innate need, an instinct, when he involves himself with images and myths of death. Jung felt, "(Man) ought to have a myth about death, for reason shows him nothing but the dark pit into which he is descending. Myth, however, can conjure up other images for him, helpful and enriching pictures of life in the land of the dead. If he believes in them, or greets them with some measure of credence, he is being just as right or just as wrong as someone who does not believe in them."[12]

Jung himself was not averse to speaking about the images and myths surrounding death, karma and reincarnation. He gladly communicated his thoughts, fantasies and dreams in conversation, in letters, and above all in the chapter, "On Life after Death," in his book, *Memories, Dreams, Reflections.* In doing so, he was, however, fully aware that he was not announcing objective knowledge or truths. On the first page of that chapter, we find: "… I have never written expressly about life after death; for then I would have had to document my ideas, and I have no way of doing that. Be that as it may, I would like to state my ideas now. Even now I can do no more than tell stories, 'mythologize.' Perhaps one has to be close to death to acquire the necessary freedom to talk about it."[13]

---

11 Ibid., p. 303.

12 *Memories,* p. 306.

13 Ibid., p. 299.

Jung was a gifted storyteller, who often let himself be carried away by the stream of his own ideas. Thus it could happen that the fascinated listener occasionally mistook his "myths" about reincarnation, karma, life after death and so forth for considered insight and passed it on as objective knowledge. It was in this way, that the criticism that Jung was less a scientist than a mystic gained support.

This misunderstanding identified him with the "mythical man" and failed to take into account that, as a researcher, he was a pure empiricist. Only by taking into consideration both sides, their complementary nature and mutual limitation, do we do justice to Jung and his work. Here, too, "Unequivocalness goes at the cost of truth."[14] Whoever overlooks this and is convinced by the objectivity of the "mythical" statements is applying the laws of the empirically understandable field of consciousness to the unfathomable transcendent, and making rational Cartesian thinking absolute. Jung expressed his view of this attitude explicitly: "If we are convinced that we know the ultimate truth concerning metaphysical things, this means nothing more than that archetypal images have taken possession of our powers of thought and feeling ... the object of perception then becomes absolute and indisputable."[15] Such a demand for absolutism leaves out the fact emphasized by Jung that the incomprehensible background of the psyche and the material per-

---

14 *Letters, II,* (June 17, 1952 Werblowsky).

15 G.W. XIV/2, p. 232 (C.W. XIV, *Mysterium Conjunctionis,* par. 787).

mits expression only in paradox and antinomy. Every assertion appears valid and invalid at the same time.[16]

Basically, Jung's view of the "mythical man" in everyone corresponds to the age-old image of the human as a dual being, as a mortal-immortal, spiritual-physical, rational-mythical being. This conception is part of man's oldest cultural heritage. It deals with a motif that, more than three thousand years ago, was described in the Indian Veda as the image of the two "closely bound friends," the one who enjoyed the world, and the other who contemplated it. It emerged in classical myth in the Dioscuri, in the image of the "two souls" in Goethe's *Faust*, and, very prosaically, as personalities numbers 1 and 2 in Jung's book, *Memories, Dreams, Reflections.* Jung lived his life as a Swiss citizen, as a father, physician and researcher, but simultaneously also as a "mythical man" in the world of imagination. The mythical man in him, number 2, led him to the creative source of timeless images, and the researcher, number 1, drew the meaningful conclusions. Within the intellectual context of the time in which he lived, he shaped these conclusions by reflecting them in his scientific work. The inner images were for him "raw material for a life's work."[17]

At this point, something else might be added from my conversations with Jung about death and the transcendent as they relate to his "myths."

---

16 Ibid., cf. p. 317 (par. 715).

17 *Memories,* p. 199.

He was, at the time of these conversations, in the ninth decade of his life and had himself experienced, as I have mentioned, that, with increasing age, reflections and the "myths of the soul" play an ever greater role. The aging person begins to search for meaningful images behind life's events and experiences. Occasionally, Jung mentioned that he regarded the world of images with which man occupies himself in the here-and-now as preliminary to a continuation of our earthly life in a "mythical existence," an existence made up of psychic images. Life after death would then be like "a moving on into the realm of images."

But man, in keeping with his mortal nature, cannot imagine existence in the hereafter as anything other than part of the sequence of events occurring in time. Basically, however, it would only appear to be a temporal sequence, just as the images of the psyche only seem to exist in space. Existence in more than four dimensions cannot be imagined at all, just as one is not able to recognize which qualities of being the psychic images possess.

Preoccupation with inner images was to Jung what philosophy was to Plato: "a preparation for death." In a way, this has the effect of preventing one from concluding one's life in retrospection. There are many elderly people who lose themselves in reminiscence. They are trapped by their memories, whereas for Jung reminiscing was only a way of "stepping back, in order to made a better leap." For him, the main thing was the attempt to recognize the line which had led into his life and into the world and which would lead out of the world again. In this, the contemplation of inner images plays an important role. His own path toward individuation mirrors this very clearly: in the very middle of his life, "the eternal images broke in."[18]

In his efforts to confront and understand these images arising from the unconscious, the words of Isaiah always came to Jung: "Your dead will live." What does this mean? Jung explained it to me in this way: "If I conceive of the image-world of the psyche as preliminary to a life after death, I could also imagine that the dead for their part live on in certain involuntary fantasies of individuals. Not in a literal sense, to be sure, but rather as structuring entities. They would thus serve the same function as the archetypes of the collective unconscious. These are also unknowable, they must be understood rather as the structuring aspect of archetypal conceptions, fantasies and images."

The dead seem to exist in a sphere to which the individual is connected through his spiritual world of images. Psychologically, this existence alludes to the unconscious psyche and its archetypal contents. In other words, what we designate as "events in the land of the dead," in the "transcendent realm," takes place in the unconscious. This corresponds to the thinking of some primitive tribes, for whom the world of dreams often means 'the land of the dead,' and this idea is not to be rejected out of hand. It seems as if the psy-

---

18 Allusion to the inner images which occupied Jung particularly in the years 1912-20, after the separation from Freud. – Cf. the chapter "Confrontation with the Unconscious," in *Memories*, p. 170 ff.

che, or rather the unconscious, is the realm, in which the dead go on living. "The unconscious is limitless, unknowable; without space and time, as the so-called 'Hereafter' is said to be limitless, and without space and time."

According to Jung, the idea that man 'chooses' his life before birth might not have come about without reason. If that were the case, one would choose the life one has imagined. If one is filled with longing one cherishes until death fantasies about things one has not lived. Out of the regret at not having done certain things, one creates one's compensations. If this were to continue according to the laws of the psyche, an impulse to realize these compensatory fantasies would be born. Jung said of himself: "I could imagine that I will compensate my present life by becoming a pioneer, but in another way than now, perhaps in the natural sciences. I understand why Buddha finally after however many incarnations did not want to return to life again. I would not go so far as to say that I would like to disappear in Nirvana. And I could imagine that a world situation could develop in which I could not help but agree to 'one more time !'" But that was not the case at this moment: he had had enough. The only thing which could have attracted him were the natural sciences, a broader knowledge of the nature of things.

"Research in the natural sciences, yes, that I could imagine as the content of a new life." But he didn't know whether this motive was sufficient. Of burning interest to him was the state of things after death, and what one could experience there, whether one needs time and space in order to have experiences. In this life, we need the experiencing ego, and the experienced object. Whether this separation continues after death is uncertain.

In Jung's opinion, everything depends on whether we possess consciousness after death and, if so, to what extent. This is the great question: whether one dies with a developed consciousness or not. Whether one then simply "is," and is blown by the great worldwind into existence again. Although the question of reincarnation appeared acceptable to him, rationally he could not understand how it could be possible. He was unable to give a definite answer.

"What grips me the most is a desire for understanding," noted Jung. In his opinion, this requires no new earthly existence. It is conceivable that in the hereafter, after death, one would have unlimited access to knowledge. It would certainly be possible, if we were to be submerged after death in a universal consciousness, in a state of being beyond opposites where the subject who experiences and the thing experienced are no longer separated. Even so, such a knowledge would not be comprehensive. For it would be information pertaining to facts and causal relationships, knowledge, so to speak, of details, not in depth. It would be an immediate knowledge of things, unlimited by time and space.

Conversely, the knowledge of that which gives one's life meaning and the insights that one gains from this life would be knowledge in depth. Increase in the details of knowledge, the acquisition of information, would be merely a means to this end.

The following dream is based upon notes that I took during Jung's own narration. They captured the unique mood and show, not least by the numerous repetitions, the effort with which Jung recovered the dream from the unconscious. His expression was distant, his voice very soft, and he interrupted the narrative several times with long periods of silence, as if he were once more immersed in that "colossal expanse," "dark distance," and strangeness that appears to characterize the borders between reality and the transcendent, consciousness and unconsciousness.

"Yesterday I had a dream that I would like to tell to you. In the dream I am on a journey, or at a train station. It was an impression that I can't quite get hold of now. Anyway, I am somehow in a foreign country and there is a large building. Perhaps the hall of a train station, or a hangar at the edge of an airfield. But there are no airplanes. A broad field stretches away in front of me at colossal distance to the horizon. A dark distance. It stretches into the infinite. There is an awareness in me that I am on a journey.

"Then comes a part of the dream that I can remember clearly. No, actually it is just as unclear. It was like this: in the background, there was a train on a track. We, a crowd of people, are standing near the locomotive, and I am with Father and Mother. I knew that they were there rather than seeing them exactly. So I was on a journey with Father and Mother and, in addition, we were in festive clothing. I know that we were coming back from a wedding that had taken place in a foreign country, far away. Father wore a top hat, and I had one too; that is, I held it in the hand in which I was also carrying my suitcase. Somewhat uncomfortable, I am thinking: how stupid, why didn't I bring a hatbox with me? I look at the top hat, which indeed looks somewhat ruffled. Mother was rather more distinct than my father and we were, as I said, on the way back from a wedding.

"I am, thus, at this point in time the son of my parents. But I was adult, more in my middle years, approximately forty years old. It was clear that we had come back from a great distance, from a cosmic distance. There was an unbelievable width and depth of space before me. And the darkness!

"Suddenly, it struck me: my sister was missing! Of course, she is the one who celebrated the wedding! So, the land from which we came must have been the beyond, or whatever that is called. During the night, I had considered every aspect of this dream and it became clear to me that this wedding could only have related to my sister.

"My sister died in her thirties. She was a remarkable person, I never had a close relationship to her. I have told you about her and her marvelous attitude. I always admired her. She died after an operation that was considered to be only minor, but she was fully aware that it was a matter of life and death.[19]

"The top hat is an amazing detail of the dream, of which I at first could make neither head

---

19 Gertrude Jung, 1884-1935. Cf. Jung, *Memories*, p. 112.

nor tail. You see, it makes the man appear taller. That is its purpose. One becomes more important, because one is taller. That is, right "there," in the place we designate as the beyond. Here, it is a hindrance, an impediment. It is really very disagreeable when one again returns to earthly conditions.

"So, we are standing on the platform beside the locomotive. I don't know: had we gotten out of the train? We walked alongside the train away from the locomotive. Presumably, we wanted to find a carriage into which we could climb. It was as if we were boarding the train in Paris or Vienna, in order to go home, but at the same time as if we had actually come from much further away.

"Now, here again, was something astonishing: Father was walking on my left and he was, or was walking, much higher than I, as if his feet were about at the height of my head. Mother was walking on my right and her feet were half as high as my father's feet. I myself had the feeling of being rather short.

"The great area of the airfield, which apparently bordered on the train station, or was identical with it, had something terrifying about it. It was dark, the beginning of night, or rather, a night-like darkness, and a space of monstrous breadth, an emptiness, a colossal emptiness. I stood just on the very edge of the field, and in front of me lay this colossal expanse, and I was engaged in 'departing' or 'arriving.'

"Now this sister in the dream is, so to speak, the personification of my unconscious, or anima. She had married. Accordingly, she must have entered into a vital bond with a masculine element. What that means for me personally, I don't know.

"I have the feeling that my tiredness during the last few days is connected with this dream experience, with this enormous distance from which I had to return. I have the feeling of a great task: I must return, must reduce the distance, "take off the top hat," get my feet back on the ground. My father had his feet at the height of my head. But somehow that was not in the air: it simply was so."

For Jung, the idea of rebirth meant "an incredibly meaningful vitalization of reality." One could characterize it directly as a "healthy fantasy" or as a "therapeutic myth." To be sure, its positive effect is not available to all, and may not be taken as a criterion of its truth. But it "suits most well" to have such, or similar, ideas about the continuation of life after death. If people had suitable images and ideas, it would make things easier; life would be more bearable, and these are "tangible advantages."

In Jung's opinion, the power of the idea of reincarnation to convince could lie in the very fact that this idea possesses a healing capacity. Whether that constitutes a proof is certainly another question. The strange healing effect inherent in this concept is evident nevertheless. But whether metaphysical events, which for us are absolutely inconceivable, proceed according to our imaginings cannot be determined, and science has been quick to use the fact that they cannot be proven as an "argument against them."

According to Eastern concepts, a human can attain certain levels of understanding from which he must not return after death, for then the continuation of a three-dimensional life would no longer have meaning. A deeper insight seems to reduce the need to reincarnate. Buddhism speaks of Nirvana, in which the individual, after a complete cessation of the instinct to live, disappears. But if a fate, a karma, still remains to be realized, then the soul recovers its desire, and enters once again into a body in order to live it out, perhaps even out of an awareness that something must still be completed. At least, this is the mythical idea.

Jung could not, and did not, want to simply brush aside the question of reincarnation: "I was internally plagued to give an answer. My intellect could not find it as it is beyond the human scope. So very early on I began to listen to what the unconscious has to say. But even if one takes the answers of the unconscious seriously, because the problem is convincingly represented in dreams, the doubt creeps in: Is that really the way it is? To that, I have nothing to say. That is a question which I cannot answer."

During a serious illness, Jung, at that time 69, had the impression of being outside his body.[20] In this condition, he was overcome by a feeling of great relief. "It was no longer a matter of youth or old age; rather, what counted was a meaningful development." Jung experienced how the element of meaning came into its own, something

20 Cf. the chapter "Visions," ibid., p. 289 ff.

that the individual perceives only darkly in his life and then so superficially that he can scarcely recognize it. "Meaning had freed itself from the bonds of the material and the Being it had become, and was able to completely unfold, blossom. 'Things' did not jostle in space any more. 'There' one has no need of time to get from one end to the other. It is a vision to end all visions. This is the *Visio Dei*. When one has experienced this with the feeling: Yes, that is it!, then there is nothing else. It is something so grand and so beautiful that the most profound peace sets in. No one can prove it invalid or nonsense."

"In the final analysis, we simply do not know whether we experience anything after death." According to Jung, a certain probability nevertheless exists that an essential part of the psyche is preserved, for the unconscious ranges into the realm that is without space and time, as parapsychological phenomena substantiate.[21] "The unconscious transcends our reality."

"I don't know how it will be, life after death. What happens to consciousness? I don't know. And that of course is the important question."

"Many myths say that, after death, the spark of the soul, the light of consciousness, flies to the sun. So it is also conceivable that, after death, consciousness is received again into a universal consciousness. Still, it remains a great mystery."

---

21 Cf. Jaffé, "Der Tod in der Sicht von C.G. Jung," op. cit., p. 22ff.